IN &
OUT
OF
SEASON

Thriving in Life's Transitions

WHAT OTHERS ARE SAYING

If you're experiencing an unexpected season, a challenging transition, a fading dream, or an unanticipated disappointment, *In & Out of Season* is the book for you. With honesty, transparency, biblical wisdom, and encouragement for your journey, Dr. Evelyn Johnson-Taylor provides what you need to make it through a temporary setback so you can begin taking important next steps. This book is filled with truth that will help you overcome fear and rediscover your purpose.
—**Carol Kent**, Founder and Director of Speak Up Ministries, speaker, author

No one plans how they will transition into seasons of grief. Dr. Evelyn Johnson-Taylor shares that though we can't plan our actions, we can respond to those seasons in a positive, life-giving way. Her Reflection sections are not too challenging for grieving souls as they supply just enough provocation to move us forward toward healing. Every library needs at least one copy of *In & Out of Season: Thriving in Life's Transitions*.
—**Linda Goldfarb**, author, speaker, podcast host, Christian life coach

Like an open book, Dr. Evelyn Johnson-Taylor shares with her readers certain phases of her life: singleness, thoughts of incompleteness, a loving marriage, family, and later becoming a widow. Dr. Johnson-Taylor shares how she has moved through her pain to fulfilling her purpose. This book is a must-read for anyone who needs encouragement and practical wisdom in navigating the seasons that are experienced in a lifetime.

—Thomas L. Dozier, PhD, Senior Pastor of The Word of Grace & Truth Ministries; President of Grace & Truth Christian University

Do you know a single who wants to marry? Or maybe your friend is confined to caring for a sick family member. Maybe, like the author, you or your friend has recently lost a beloved spouse. Just as each year contains different seasons, so each life passes through different times. Drawing from her personal life story, Evelyn Johnson-Taylor reminds us that God is always with us. And if we trust him, we'll bear fruit and find joy even in our harshest winters. *In & Out of Season* is the book you'll reach for when you or someone you love needs hope.

—Debbie W. Wilson, author

Dr. Johnson-Taylor cuts a clear path through the enigmatic curtains of life, revealing a clear reality for those who will transverse the inevitable seasons of life. *In & Out of Season* is a reflective and riveting treatise on the effects of loss. Dr. Johnson-Taylor's writing is crisp, clean, and poignant as she takes you on a vivid journey to help you cross the many bridges of transition in our unique journeys.

—Bishop Derek L. Calhoun, M.Div., author, co-founder and overseer of New Vision International Ministries

If only life did not include painful transitions. Sadly, it does. No life is spared. With incredible sensitivity and beautifully inspiring prose, Evelyn Johnson-Taylor shares her journey through tumultuous transitions. From the first page, I cared deeply about her as she wove her true love story with such skill she had me spellbound. Along the journey, I celebrated her love and felt deep compassion for her heart-crushing hardships and loss. But Evelyn is living proof that all is not lost. Her family's legacy of faith, instilled in her from birth, is the groundwork that allows her to step with grace and confidence throughout her life, from one transition to the next. Skillfully, she lays the structure of how faith allowed her to move through unimaginable hardships and lifted her spirit to glorify God in all things.

In & Out of Season: Thriving in Life's Transitions will hook you from the first page and teach a path, like grounded stepping stones, to pilot you through the rocky waters of your own transitions.

—Deborah McCormick Maxey PhD, professional counselor, marriage and family therapist, author

Powerful and poignant! The seasons of life can offer challenges we never dreamed possible. However, there is hope when we remind ourselves of the faithfulness of God. With beautiful transparency, Dr. Evelyn Johnson-Taylor gently shows her readers how to navigate life's most difficult transitions. If you are in any challenging season, this is your book! You will feel as though you have a personal friend on your journey. I highly recommend it!

—Becky Harling, speaker, coach, author, certified coach with the John Maxwell Team

My grandmother wistfully repeated, "The only constant is change." Dr. Johnson-Taylor has given us a guidebook for the changes in our lives whether celebratory or devastating. With sound wisdom sprinkled with her quiet wit, she reminds us we never face this life alone but are always guided by our great God of grace. For any change you are facing, I highly recommend this resource to help carry you through!

—Erica Wiggenhorn, speaker, author

It should not matter whether you are chosen to make a change in the lives of people. What should matter is that you are obedient to whatever God has called you to do! I have personally walked with Dr. Johnson-Taylor through her obedience in writing her numerous books. This book reflects the reality she has lived, and others have yet to live. Through her written words that offer clear advice people will be enabled to gain control over what has the potential to destroy them.

—**Clarise H. Ottley**, **PhD,** Women's Empowerment Leadership Ministry, professional development counselor, author

Dr. Johnson-Taylor's work is a relevant book for women experiencing a need for lifestyle modification in any season of life. Evelyn's life with Scott provides wholesome hope for the reader during transitions of career decisions, singleness, marriage, and death with spiritual direction. The voice of wisdom penned to be embraced for one to gain determination to live and believe again.

—**Dr. Karynthia A.G. Phillips**, author, speaker, CEO/Founder of Echoes of Hope, Inc.

There are seasons of life that take our breath. Author Dr. Evelyn Johnson-Taylor has experienced love, joy, and the shock of fierce transitions. When change means your heart may never be the same, Johnson-Taylor is your compassionate companion, assuring that God is at work for your best even in this.

—**PeggySue Wells,** author, speaker, writing coach

IN & OUT OF SEASON

Thriving in Life's Transitions

EVELYN JOHNSON-TAYLOR, PhD

ELK LAKE PUBLISHING INC.®

PUBLISHING THE POSITIVE
Plymouth, Massachusetts

A Christian Company
ElkLakePublishingInc.com

COPYRIGHT NOTICE

Library Cataloging Data

Names: Johnson-Taylor, Evelyn (Evelyn Johnson-Taylor)
In and Out of Season: Thriving in Life's Transitions / Evelyn, Johnson-Taylor

182 p. 23 cm × 15 cm (9 in. × 6 in.)

ISBN-13: 9798891342408 (paperback) | 9798891342415 (trade paperback) | 9798891342422 (e-book)

Key Words: Christian women's self-help death of loved one; Jesus recovery illness divorce death for women; Christian living loss bereavement renewal; Season of change Christ comfort for women; Death and grief coping journey Christian women; Renewed identity God women after death divorce; Spirituality faith widowed healing faith hope

Library of Congress Control Number: 2024945570 Nonfiction

DEDICATION

I dedicate this book to the memory of my husband, Scott Barry Taylor, in appreciation of all he poured into my life and all that his absence has taught me.

09/23/1959–06/20/2018.

Table of Contents

FOREWORD

Transitions. Change. Upheaval.

None of these conditions are something we seek out or look forward to. Instead, each one is a struggle common to everyone. Most of us go to great lengths to avoid them, and yet, through these times of challenge, we can find riches beyond imagining.

Dr. Evelyn Johnson-Taylor knows what it's like to endure transition—and come through it with a stronger faith, a deeper relationship with God, and a better understanding of who God created her to be. Her willingness to share the insight she's gained through the journey will help each of us as we travel this path.

This book is organized like the best kind of travel guidebook. Not only does Evelyn provide a map, forged from her own personal experiences and a strong foundation of Scripture, she includes notes about any side trips the reader may take.

Included are chapters on how personality affects the process, what to do with disappointment, and the preparation process. Dr. Johnson-Taylor doesn't neglect the process of moving from a struggle into ministry. And she addresses fear, freedom, and acceptance.

The one thing missing from this book is ego. There is nothing from the author that feels like she's claiming to have all the answers. Instead, she constantly points the reader to God, simply allowing her experiences to illustrate the truth we can find in Scripture.

Each chapter includes an application with well-researched Scripture, a reflection to help the reader think through his or her own story, and a prayer to help the reader process while walking with God.

This is a book to cherish, letting God bring you through the chaos and into the fullness of His love and peace.

Blessings,

Edie Melson, Director of the Blue Ridge Mountains Christian Writers Conference

ACKNOWLEDGMENTS

I want to express my appreciation to Peggy Sue Wells who did the first-line review of this manuscript. To Deb Haggerty, Judy Hagey, the team at Elk Lake Publishing, and especially my editor, Paul Conant, thank you. When my manuscript was accepted for publication, I prayed, asking God to connect me with the right editor.

To everyone who wrote an endorsement for this book, and my Value of a Season Group, thank you. Your unwavering support and belief in this project encouraged me to continue writing when thoughts of quitting arose.

I am deeply humbled and blessed by the prospect of how God will utilize the words within these pages to reach and uplift readers. All glory is attributed to my heavenly Father.

INTRODUCTION

Nothing and no one remain the same.

The cycle of life is always in motion, just like the cycle of the four seasons. As the days become longer and the weather warmer, spring brings the chance to sow new seeds and bring life to the garden. During summer, the branches of trees are full of luscious fruits, waiting to be gathered. The fall brings a flurry of activity to the fields as farmers harvest the crops they carefully tended all season. Some plants rely on the frigid winter temperatures to become dormant and store energy for the fresh growth of spring. There is value in every season.

Change is a fundamental part of life and something we can detect, encounter, and observe in the alternating periods of the year and life. The four distinct climates offer a variety of unique experiences, and similarly, life's seasons allow the opportunity to plant, nurture, harvest, and start again.

Season refers to four divisions of the year: spring, summer, fall, and winter. Some areas have humid summers and snowy winters. In autumn, the temperature may dip. There are places where leaves turn to shades of yellow, orange, and red, which is a sign that one season is about to pass.

Though the traditional patterns are absent in Florida where I live, the air feels different, signaling the change in season. When I reached the age of fifty, I entered a new season of life. Soon enough my body would tell me this was so.

In the Tanakh, Ecclesiastes 3:1 reads, "A season is set for everything, a time for every experience under heaven."[1] Each aspect of life has a prearranged time. Events, whether good or bad, have their own designated time to occur. The concept of time is inextricably linked to the divine nature of God.

In Galatians 6:9, Paul writes, "And let us not grow weary of doing good, for in due season we will reap, if we do not give up." In this Scripture, the word season refers to the right time, an opportune time, or seasonable time. Paul encourages the Galatians to keep giving as God promised at the proper time to reward those who are faithful.

Each phase of life from childhood to youth, from adult to senior citizen offers something new to take in, an invitation to sow with excitement to reap the rewards when the time is right. With the changing of the seasons, we are reminded of the joyous feeling of laughter and the sadness that comes with tears. Gray skies with rain and days of sunshine are equally important to achieve the vibrant blooming of flowers and the juicy plumping of vegetables.

Unplanned modifications, like losing a loved one, can be overwhelmingly difficult and cause life to spiral into chaos. A transition is defined as "a change or shift from one state, subject, place, etc. to another, a period or phase in which such a change or shift is happening."[2] In life, people experience modifications of many kinds—job loss, marriage, starting a family, and the death of a loved one.

Despite our resistance, changes inevitably come. Some major life changes are planned such as going to college, getting married, and having children, but even with the best of intentions, moving between stages of life can be challenging. This book is not only about learning how to cope with difficult times but how to blossom in those times. Difficult seasons can be a source of strength, teaching valuable lessons about having faith, never giving up hope, developing patience, and learning to forgive.

We all have paths we'd rather not go down and seasons we prefer not to experience. With God by my side, I set out on a journey to learn the wisdom that life offered me as a widow.

–CHAPTER 1–
PASSAGE THROUGH PAIN

"I'm a widow," I whispered to my friend as we left the emergency room, not wanting to say the words too loud for fear the volume would make them true. For ten years, I had been Scott's caregiver. The notion had crossed my mind that I might one day be a widow ... but not today.

"Give him something for the pain," I said to the emergency room doctor. "Then I will take him home."

The doctor shook her head. "He's not going home today."

That was just one hour ago.

The doctor and I were both wrong. Scott did go home that day, but not with me. He went to his heavenly home to be with the Lord.

When moments before the room was alive with activity, the hustle and bustle abruptly stopped. All the noise faded away. My heart pounded a drumbeat in my chest.

I couldn't take my eyes off my husband's lifeless body. My heart yearned for one more chance to tell him the things I wanted to say. Despite the longevity of his illness, I freely sacrificed to care for him. I needed Scott to know we would miss him. That I loved him.

But none of those things mattered to him anymore. Scott was finally at peace. But how could he be happy anywhere that wasn't with me?

"I hate to leave my family," Scott often told me. "I loved you from the first time we talked."

He dedicated his life to making sure we had everything we needed. Never asking for much in return, he was a giver.

"You know what I enjoy most?" He had reached for my hand. "Being with my family."

The decision to end medical tests and procedures did not come easy. He wanted to stay with us as long as possible. But the time had come. He felt exhausted and ready to rest.

I enjoyed being married; belonging to someone made me feel safe. Now I was alone. In a split second, my life changed forever.

Just a few weeks prior, we celebrated our twenty-seventh wedding anniversary. Eager to make me smile, Scott deferred to me to choose the restaurant.

"You choose," I said.

He shook his head.

A few days earlier, our daughter spent Father's Day with him, although we didn't know this one would be his last.

The day started unremarkably, like the ones that came before. Why didn't I receive some unction this day would be his last with me? I shook my head in disbelief as we stepped into the hospital parking lot. The day was hot, typical of Florida in late June. People continued with their activities, but everything changed for me that day.

"I'll drive." My friend reached for my car keys.

As I rode in the passenger seat, tears coursed down my cheeks. Over and over, like the rhythm of a song, my thoughts repeated, "I am a widow."

Maybe I was ready to do all the things required of a surviving spouse. After all, I already managed our finances, the home, medical matters, and our limited social life. "It wouldn't be that hard," I reasoned.

I was wrong.

Scott and I discussed death more than the average couple, I'm sure. Because of our faith, neither of us was afraid. We imagined heaven and being with Jesus. We dreamed of a life away from the hospital and without physical pain. After Scott's multiple close brushes with death, I believed I would sense when the time for him to pass drew near. Surely, I would have an impression signaling this vital transition for my husband.

But I didn't. If there were clues, I did not recognize them.

Despite asking God to remove the pain or take him home, Scott stayed and made the best of this rugged situation. I didn't expect him to leave me today.

Can anyone be ready for such a significant loss? I didn't want to do life without Scott by my side. I didn't want to be alone.

Back home, surrounded by friends and neighbors, a fleeting relief washed over me—Scott would no longer endure pain. For years, my constant concern had been who would care for Scott if I were unable. He would never need my care again because he was with the Master Caregiver, resting in the arms of a loving and faithful God. I exhaled, knowing if I became sick or died, there was no longer a need to arrange for his care. God answered Scott's prayers and called him home.

Then fear quickly swept in. What about me? My husband no longer needed me, but I needed him.

Several weeks earlier, his doctors said Scott's heart was in critical condition. Chemotherapy treatments exacerbated the results of the rheumatic fever he suffered as a child, leaving his heart valves vulnerable. Scott underwent a cardiac catheterization while under local anesthesia because of his low blood pressure. The heart stents came with the hope of another six months, and we quietly trusted God for a miracle as we left the hospital.

There were no outward signs of deteriorating health, so I didn't allow myself to dwell on the negative report.

One month after his discharge from the hospital, Scott commented, "I feel the same. Maybe the doctors were wrong."

I now believe he experienced a version of *terminal lucidity*. This is when an ill person gets a period of increased energy days before they pass away. His comment gave both of us hope. Scott's condition had mystified doctors many times before. Could it be he was going to bewilder them again?

He complained of chest pain just hours before his death, so I persuaded him to let me call an ambulance.

My sister asked, "Do you want to ride with him?"

"No, I'll drive myself." I'd called an ambulance for Scott before. Why would this day be any different? "Can you lock the doors for me?"

His hospitalizations over the past decade were too many to count. We both knew the drill. If they admitted him, I'd get him settled in his room, come home for the night, and visit him again the next day. In the early days of his illness, with every hospitalization, I'd check in with him. Later, I tried to use his admissions as a respite for me. We had our routine at home, but in the hospital, his medication, meals, and sleep schedule led to irritability for both of us.

Scott's death thrust me into a new stage of life, and I wasn't ready. What would this transition mean for me? How would the absence of their father affect our young adult daughters? Their father listened to them, laughed at their jokes, and watched their favorite television shows even when they weren't home.

He introduced them to musicals. When they were four and six years old, he took them to see *Annie*. That was the beginning of a shared love affair for the arts that would last for the rest of his life. "I recorded this for you," he'd say when they came home from college. Doing things the girls enjoyed made him feel closer to them, even when they were not at home.

Our youngest daughter joked, "You make us feel like your life only began when we were born."

Would our daughters be okay without their dad? Would I? What was next?

Scott had asked multiple times, "Will you be all right after I'm gone?"

At that moment, I wasn't sure I'd ever be okay again. *Oh, God, what now?*

REFLECTION

What is your story? What transition are you going through that prompted you to pick up this book?

PRAYER

Oh, God. Oh, God. Oh, God.

Father, thank you for the answer when I don't know what to ask. When I don't have the words. You are the loving Father who knows what I need before I ask. You hear my call, even when my prayer is only two words. Though my husband is not with me, you promised to never leave or forsake me. Though a surprise to me, Scott's death was not a surprise to you. Lord. don't leave me now. You answer "Oh, God" prayers.

–CHAPTER 2–
PERSONALITY IMPACTS TRANSITIONS

Much of childhood defines who we become as adults. Mother's stories of our childhood often included Daddy carrying us to bed on late Sunday nights, exhausted after another long day.

Sunday was anything but a day of rest. Preparations began the night before. Clothes laid out, baths finished, and devotions read. The lights were turned off, and we children were in bed early, at times even before darkness set in. The morning drive to church took an hour, and we had to be up early. Being on time was a priority for my father. The word *late* was not in his vocabulary.

Daddy wanted to be sure the church building was warm in the winter and cool in the summer when the parishioners arrived. We were accustomed to hearing the sound of the car horn on Sunday morning, so it wasn't anything new to us. Running out the door to get into the idling car headed to church resembled school days when I ran to catch the bus.

None of us wanted to be last in the car. Dad was always first. That Sunday, twenty minutes into our drive, I realized I didn't have my church shoes. Shaking his head and sighing loudly, Dad turned back to the house. My mistake threw off his rhythm, but we survived, and the world didn't end because someone arrived at church before us.

Sunday was the longest day of our week. First, there was Sunday school, then morning service. We'd return to church for Sunday evening services after a long afternoon with a kind family who hosted the pastor and his family for lunch.

We loved spending Sundays with a family that had kids our age, because we got to play and enjoy a meal together. Once the adults had finished eating, the children could take their turn. As soon as we finished our meal, we rolled up our sleeves and volunteered to help clean the kitchen. We were grateful for their hospitality and wanted to show our appreciation by doing something, even if it was just a small gesture.

As an adult, I see how much of the way I deal with loss, grief, trauma, and disappointment is linked to how I processed things as a child. Some perceived me as an overthinker who required careful consideration of strategies before expressing thoughts. Not much has changed, I still like to "sleep on it" before making any decision.

As we consider how our childhood relates to adulthood, we need to look at identifying characteristics. Identity deals with the distinguishing character or personality trait of an individual. Our identity is composed of a set of physical, emotional, and interpersonal characteristics. These behaviors define who we are, the way we think about ourselves, how we intermingle with others, and how others view us.

Parental relationships, boundaries, and forms of discipline received from our environment, combined with our inherited temperament, impact how we view ourselves and how we respond to others. Tim LaHaye writes in Transforming Your Temperament that "temperament is the combination of inborn traits that subconsciously affect man's behavior. These traits are arranged genetically on the basis of nationality, race, sex, and other hereditary factors. These traits are passed on by the genes."1

Those long drives to church caused me to make an inner vow never to be a part of a church more than thirty minutes from where I lived. I imposed similar limits in other areas of my life. Intentionally setting limits can help you maintain balance and structure while focusing on your top priorities. Establishing limits, however, can have some negative consequences or drawbacks. Instead of feeling relieved, my strict boundaries caused me to feel more stressed and anxious. I wanted to control my environment. By not allowing space for mistakes or learning experiences, I missed out on opportunities that could have facilitated personal growth.

The pressure to meet strict limits detracted me from the enjoyment of some experiences because I was preoccupied with rules and restrictions rather than fully engaging in the moment. I became rigid and inflexible. This can be problematic when dealing with changing circumstances or when adaptation to a new season is necessary.

A respected community leader, Daddy's generosity extended far beyond our home. Our church was small, and there weren't a lot of finances or outreach programs. When people couldn't pay their bills, they called Daddy. When someone was ill, they called the pastor. Regardless of the hour, Daddy had a passion for helping as many people as he could regardless of the day of the week.

Late at night, the phone would ring. Something must be wrong. Our parents quietly left the house to assist someone experiencing an emergency. They were available when someone needed marrying or burying and everything in between.

Although my parents' heavy involvement with ministry appeared demanding, I never felt neglected as a child. When I was born, Daddy was already a preacher. It all seemed normal to me. Didn't everybody's parents slip out of the house in the middle of the night to help someone in need?

Daddy's role in the church imposed certain limitations. Our Pentecostal upbringing restricted us from going to the movies or dancing. Girls couldn't wear pants, makeup, or jewelry. People expected us to be active in the church.

In my early years, we lived with Grandma, so we didn't have to go to church every time our parents went. By the time Grandma died, we were old enough to stay home alone and didn't have to go to midweek services.

Young and naïve, I vowed my children would never feel the restrictions of limited social interaction. My future husband and I would add exciting and fresh experiences to their itinerary. As parents, we would encourage our children to enjoy activities, and if my children had homework, I would stay home to help them with it.

Kids at school called me "PK" for preacher's kid, remarking that preachers have the worst troublemakers. I knew some preacher's kids who got into trouble, but so did the deacon's kids, the choir director's kids, the Sunday school teacher's kids, and the kids of congregational members.

My firmly melancholy state of mind with perfectionist leanings drove me to prove them wrong. I was so determined to meet my standards that I struggled to open my heart and accept God's grace of forgiveness. To prove my value, I strove to make sure nobody believed I was unreliable or inadequate.

Serving God's people with intentionality was what my father demonstrated. His level of integrity showed me the meaning of commitment, punctuality, and keeping my word. Determined to be above reproach, I focused on my performance and what impression others might take away. Doing things according to my inner measurement of what was right, I often questioned what could have been if I had taken different paths. Rethinking what I "should have done" resulted in feelings of guilt. Mentally, I lived in the past or worried about the future rather than being in the present.

As an adult and with Scott's help, I toiled to reconstruct my thought process. He helped me become aware of how my personality responded to my environment and the inner messages and vows I made in response.

When our children were born, I could see each girl had their own unique personality. Our first daughter was born with a head full of jet-black hair. Although she was also born with pneumonia, her cry was louder than the other babies in the nursery. I heard her screams echoing down the hallway before she reached my room at feeding time. From birth, our baby girl displayed a strong and confident personality.

Being alone was not her cup of tea; she loved social interaction. "Can you please read to me? I'm bored. Would you like to play a game with me? What are you doing? When will Dad be home?" The incessant questioning continued without pause. "Asking questions is a good thing," Granddad said with a smile. The good thing was he didn't have to deal with answering all of them.

The authors of Linked: Maximizing Life Connections One Link at a Time write that "some personality traits begin to exhibit themselves in infancy and toddlerhood."[2] I sensed in those early days our baby girl would have her dad's tendency for theatrics.

She was a natural for acting—her stage presence captivated audiences. We encouraged her to explore art and the theater and fostered her passion as she joined the show choir at her school. She gravitated to the spotlight.

Our youngest daughter was a calm baby, quite the opposite of her sister. If someone looked at her too long, tears flowed down her perfectly shaped face. She was a happy baby at home but didn't take easily to others. Observant, she was a thinker, like me. Despite the shortness of her words, the weight of their meaning was substantial. She needed more than a simple yes or no answer—she needed to know the reasons behind the decision.

Playing alone was something that came easily to her right from the beginning. Although she didn't ask "When is Dad coming home?" she'd always be the first to greet him at the door and would get upset if someone else ran ahead of her.

Scott's passing created an immense void in our family. According to their natural personalities, my daughters responded differently to this jolting transition. How could I come alongside each of them to ease their grief while I felt overwhelmed by my own? His death made me question my worth and purpose. I pressed my hands to my head, puzzled at the thought, "What do I do now?" For twenty-seven years, I had been his wife. For the last decade, I had been devoted to being his caregiver. What was I to do now that I was no longer Mrs.?

RESPONSE TO TRANSITION

The way people deal with transition varies. Our response is as unique as we are. We sometimes pause in the face of transitions, while other times we glide through. A transition or occurrence doesn't have to define us, but what I learn about myself and God better prepares me for the future.

Leaving the hospital on that pivotal day triggered a period of intense questioning and doubt about my purpose and worth in life. As I was no longer Scott's caretaker, his death changed me. Yet at the core, I remained the same person. My identity wasn't solely defined by my relationship with my husband. While his passing undoubtedly impacted my life significantly, I still had the capacity to rediscover myself, heal, and find new sources of meaning and purpose.

God's love for me wasn't because I took care of my husband. The understanding that God's love isn't conditional upon my actions or roles, but is rather based on the fact I am his child is liberating and calming. This powerful realization about my worth and God's plans for me confirmed I was heading in the right direction.

I am who I am today because of every experience. The unenjoyable ones were necessary to my development as a woman of faith. Everything I've faced has prepared me to encourage others. I've seen enough endings to my stories to know God's faithfulness is undeniable.

When I experienced an existential crisis, life events jolted my perception and produced questions. Christian Counselor Gary Collins, PhD, said, "Existential crises are struggles that occur when people are forced to face disturbing questions about themselves such as 'Who am I?' or 'What is my life purpose now?' Some people are resilient in times of crisis. There is evidence that resilience can be taught."[3]

One thing that helped me was to connect with others. I needed people to come alongside me to assist me with things I could not do for myself. Although I am a private person, I had to be open to letting others in. I found it difficult to trust my judgment when handling financial matters, so I had to be open to letting someone I trusted advise me. Crises can be a time when truths are revealed about us and others. The peaceful coexistence I had maintained was shattered, and the truths I had hidden for so long were exposed. I felt a knot in my stomach as I acknowledged my secret insecurities and knew I had to work through them. Without Scott, I felt lost in social situations, no longer having his outgoing personality to lean on.

Coping with an existential crisis was challenging, but I found solace and direction through my faith. I constantly reminded myself that God's plan for me remained intact. However, knowing this did not lessen the difficulty of the situation. I had to experience the transition and everything this massive change brought.

Personality and Identity

Nature or nurture? Our personality influences how we respond to our environment, events, and experiences. Environment, events, and experiences impact identity.

Life consists of unexpected turns and complications, many perplexing and devastatingly sad. Predisposing factors determine how you handle transitions including your self-perception and what you believe about your identity. Your speech serves as a window into your inner self.

After Scott's death, my overwhelming insecurity left me believing I'd decide nothing with confidence again. My personality responded to self-imposed childhood pressures of vowing to do everything right. To remain beyond reproach. Without Scott, what if a decision I made was wrong? Who would stand by me? Even though I made most of the decisions while he was ill, I would now be without his encouraging words.

The Scriptures are full of examples that highlight the power of words, showing how they can shape our identity. Jesus said in Matthew 15:11, "It is not what goes into the mouth that defiles a person, but what comes out of the mouth; this defiles a person." Here Jesus addresses the wrong thinking of the religious leaders. The words that come from the mouth reflect what is in the heart. Negativity comes from the inside, not the outside.

I made a conscious effort to embrace the idea that making mistakes is a normal component of existence. I shifted my mindset to regard them as acceptable and even valuable experiences in my journey to redefine myself in my new role. I needed to adjust my inner dialogue, focusing on gratitude and self-compassion.

Language can influence life trajectories. Believing lies spoken by yourself or others causes a crisis in identity. In crisis, we vacillate between what we think about ourselves and who God says we are.

What words do you use to describe yourself? What words do others use regarding you that have become your truth?

Whether your current identity is a child, parent, spouse, or widow, the core of who God created you to be is somewhere among the debris of the transitions you've experienced. When I saw widowed friends, I fought hard to avoid comparing my journey to theirs. Some of them seemed to have great success in their professional lives while still grieving. Looking from the sidelines, I admired the strong network of friends supporting them. Despite the loss of their husbands, they exuded a sense of confidence that I desperately desired but lacked.

I started to notice that women who maintain their independence and sense of self appear to be more resilient in the face of challenging life events, like death or divorce. As I pondered, I asked myself if the lens of grief influenced my perception. My grief counselor said a job was a blessing when dealing with grief. It gives you something else to focus on. But I experienced a double loss. My husband died and I lost my job at the same time. My daily mantra became one of missing my husband.

Some aspects of identity are temporary. Being a toddler or student is short-term. Relationship status lasts as long as the relationship. These interactions and interconnections with others affect how we feel about ourselves and influence the vows we make to ourselves. If you've said, "I'll never do that again" or "I will always ...," you've typically made inner vows in reaction to an experience.

Crises and transitions often spotlight inner vows. When I recognized my inner vows, I was able to renounce them. I didn't want to narrow my resolve by not releasing myself from an inner vow. I knew it would hold me back. Inner vows made because of a thought, word, or action associated with our past can hinder our advancement. Growth practices adopted in reaction to nature and nurture are valuable to our development and can aid in forming a temporary identity. The key is to recognize and accept the value God puts on us because that is our authentic self.

Before you knew him or loved him, he knew you. Whether you ever choose to know or love him, God loved you so much he sent his only Son to pay the price for your sins and establish an everlasting relationship with you (John 3:16–17). While our personality is not defined by one thing, but influenced by nature, nurture, and experience, our value to Creator God is beyond measure.

Can you remain your authentic self no matter how much life changes?

REFLECTION

How did you get to where you are today? How did your moral compass develop? Why do you believe what you believe? What inner vows have you made and how do they hold you back?

Examine these questions with an honest and reflective attitude and you can uncover the basic qualities of who God made you to be. Our successes and failures will shape our path ahead. Our attitude towards change determines how we will approach an unfamiliar experience. We may think we know how we would react until we are actually in the middle of the change; however, we can never be certain until we experience it. The mission is to not let any experience go to waste, no matter how enjoyable or unpleasant the incident may be.

In this transition to life without my husband, my mind was foggy like a cloud of confusion had descended upon me. Doing simple tasks was exhausting. Could I adjust to my new life without Scott?

PRAYER

Dear Father,

Thank you for the time I had with my spouse. We went through many seasons together. Life is different without my husband, but I must carry on. I need strength to continue. In times of loneliness, comfort my heart. In times of lack, please provide.

I don't understand why things happen, but I trust you know the plans you have for my life. Heal my sad heart and renew my mind. Help me dream again, knowing that because I am still here, my purpose is not complete.

Comfort me as I experience grief. I ask for your presence and love to consume me. Lead and guide me, Lord, to not waste any experience or encounter as I go through the various times of life. God, please give me the grace needed to endure what lies before me. I trust you, Father, with my future. I don't know what tomorrow holds, but I know who holds tomorrow. Amen.

–CHAPTER 3–
TRANSITIONS CAN BE DISAPPOINTING

"Do I listen to you when you need me to?"

Coaxed by my life coach, I did a self-evaluation with the goal of improving my relationships. I asked a trusted friend to be honest. "Am I a good friend?"

"You overthink things," my friend responded. "You put way too much pressure on yourself."

She knew me well. I regularly put a lot of pressure on myself based on what I thought people expected, when in reality, my assumptions were most likely far from the truth. When I understood the function of each relationship, I reduced expectations, avoiding letdowns and disappointment.

Friends have a role. Understanding the reason for their presence helped me better control what I expected. How unhealthy it is to ask for something my friend can't provide or hold my friend accountable for something they shouldn't be accountable for.

As I approached my twenty-fifth birthday, most of my friends were getting married; I wanted to be loved and in love. I too wanted to plan a future with someone wonderful. As my milestone birthday grew closer, I felt great anxiety. I couldn't shake the emptiness I felt and the loneliness of my unanswered prayers for a husband. With no tangible prospects, I spiraled into discouragement and negative self-talk.

My sister understood and hosted a birthday celebration to make me feel better. For her little sister's milestone birthday, she wanted to create an extra special day, filled with plenty of love and appreciation. I could feel my anticipation growing as I showed up for the party.

I'd moved to the area a few months earlier and still felt like an outsider. Within a few days, I found an apartment and a job near the church I attended. Though I had achieved much of what I set out to do, instead of focusing on my accomplishments, I fixated on comments asking when I would be married. I had met nice men, but none of them was the one God intended for me.

"Don't be so picky," well-meaning friends advised. Their words left me feeling uncertain. Was I outside of the will of God? Was being single God's plan for me? Why was God not answering my prayer for a husband? Their disapproval fueled my doubts.

My goals seemed doable on paper. I had a job as a registered nurse at a small, nearly one-hundred-year-old hospital. Conveniently located on Capitol Hill, the facility was close to restaurants, shopping, and museums. Instead of going to the gym after work, some days my friend Karen and I jogged to the National Mall. One of my favorite spots was the Lincoln Memorial Reflecting Pool. With walking paths and shade trees on both sides, this felt like the ideal place to unwind after my twelve-hour shift.

In the spring, tourists flock to the nation's capital every year to see the cherry blossom trees in bloom. With employee underground parking available to me at the hospital, I parked my car there and walked. Finding the best viewing spots for the annual parade wasn't a problem. I discovered the nation's capital to be an exciting place to live and work.

Every time there was a Bible study night, I left work and made my way to the church where a diverse group of male and female young professionals attended. We spent time together outside of church events. On weekends and holidays, whoever made dinner invited the rest of us over. If no one cooked, we went out. There was always someone to do something with.

Despite all this, how could I be sad and feel so unfulfilled and lonely? By whose standards did I measure myself? I had many reasons to celebrate, but each wedding invitation from a friend was a reminder. I felt I should have either been engaged or married. The fact I was still single left me anxious. Had God decided marriage was not in my future? I prayed, but when was God going to answer? Possibly, he had already answered. Perhaps his answer was no.

REFOCUS

Consumed with self-pity, I could taste the sourness of my perceived failure. I directed my attention toward my single status instead of the potential accomplishments I could achieve while waiting. Preoccupied with what I might be missing, I didn't appreciate what was currently transpiring. Because I labeled the situation as a disappointment, I missed an opportunity to discover possibilities.

Similarly, in Luke 24:19–35, the disciples expressed disappointment after the crucifixion of Jesus. Feeling dejected and let down, they confided in a stranger they met on the road to Emmaus. Jesus was the one they expected to redeem Israel, but then he died. The disciples failed to recognize Jesus's mission would be achieved, just not in the way they expected. Jesus took them back to the words of the prophets. He reminded them that for the Messiah to enter into his glory, he must first suffer these things (24:26).

Like the disciples, I expected God to do things the way I thought they should be done. I had focused on the promises in God's Word while ignoring the process of receiving them. Not being married made me blind to my true identity before I met Scott. I methodically and mistakenly gauged my worth by my current situation. After all, despite my faith, God answered differently than I thought he would.

We can offer our prayers for a desired outcome while understanding God is in control. Taking the time to recognize and savor even minor successes can bring much joy. God has strategically designed every detail of our lives. There will be bumps on the road of life. We will inevitably take wrong turns along the way. Some distractions we encounter will be self-imposed while others are God-designed. Discerning the differences between the two is beneficial.

My situation did not immediately change. Yet, as he did with the disciples on the road to Emmaus, Jesus walked with me in my disappointed state. The hearts of the disciples burned when he explained the Scriptures to them. The truth of God's Word encouraged them in what appeared to be their most disappointing season. Even though they failed to recognize him, Jesus was in their midst to ease their disappointment.

Disappointed and discouraged, I carried a heavy burden on my heart, clouding my vision of the presence of the almighty God. When I sat in his presence, I felt the peace and joy of knowing my Father was holding my hand and was with me every step of the way. Recognizing God has a plan for us gives us strength and courage to have hope and faith in him.

MIRROR, MIRROR

Examining my image in the mirror, I was determined to break away from the complaining, ungrateful person reflected in the glass. Instead of focusing on what was missing, the time had come to concentrate on making the most of the season I was in. I discovered if I cultivated open-mindedness, I could more easily adjust to different circumstances and outcomes even when they might not be what I hoped for.

As soon as I surrendered my expectations to God and put my faith in him, life became more rewarding. I disregarded the stigma of what age was acceptable for me to marry. I still had the ambition of getting married, yet I knew meeting the right man was not the only thing I should focus on in my life. That was in God's hands. I no longer lived in a "when" state: "I will do this when that happens." Instead, I resolved to live in the present.

I refused to accept I was past my prime for getting married or that I was an old maid. I was adamant about not allowing other people's opinions to sway my convictions about where I should be in life and what I should be doing. God knew the plans he had for me, and they were good. Focusing on my present mission was where my energy rested.

Each night, I listed the things I felt thankful for in my gratitude journal. Posting notes of Scripture affirmations on my bathroom mirror reminded me of what God said about me. Psalm 139:14 declares, "I praise you, for I am fearfully and wonderfully made. Wonderful are your works; my soul knows it very well."

When I wanted to express disapproval of myself, Scripture told me differently. Taking in the beauty of the person God created caused me to rethink the words I used to describe myself.

No longer willing to miss what God had for me in this season of my life, I learned no matter what I was going through, I was born with a purpose. I wasn't an accident but deliberately planned and placed on earth at a certain time in history for a purpose. The fact things hadn't happened on my schedule did not disqualify me from what God had for me in my future. When the voice in my head wanted me to believe I had missed God's plan, I countered with the Word of God. My marital status did not define my identity.

One's relationship status is a temporary season. I trusted God's grander plan for me. Initially, this period seemed dry and unproductive. Then, doing things I enjoyed became a priority. I loved time with friends, shopping, savoring scrumptious meals from fine restaurants, traveling, and taking part in activities. Realizing I could be content on my own, I discovered God had graciously provided the resources to do what he planned in each stage. Viewing my blessings instead of disappointments, I saw new opportunities.

I understood that even if marriage was not in my future, the most important thing was to align myself with God's plan for my life as a single woman. I asked God to help me be useful in my current status, and I submitted to that process. My goal was to live each day according to God's will. Though my status remained unchanged, and I remained single for several years, I changed. I adapted to a new thought process while in an unchanged season.

God taught me the opinions of others had no impact on his plan for my life. Armed with this knowledge, I decided which voices to listen to and which ones to ignore. Once I put these relationship boundaries in place, I felt confident God could use me in every term of life if I was willing. I knew what I learned in those days would better equip me for the times to follow.

New Opportunities

Waiting for God's promises prepared me to walk through doors he would open during upcoming seasons in my life. As a single, I

- was only responsible for me and what I needed.
- was free to do what I wanted with my money.
- could be active in my church.
- had time to focus on building my career.
- could be active in the District of Columbia Nurses Union.

Later, as president of this organization at the hospital where I worked, I testified before a committee representing nurses on matters related to what became the Family Leave Act. At the bargaining table until the wee hours of the night, I knew failure to agree risked a strike. I had interviews on the radio, saw my name in the newspapers, and marched with Reverend Jesse Jackson.

None of those were on my list of goals to accomplish, but taking on these additional responsibilities increased my self-confidence. As my sphere of influence enlarged, I developed talents and gifts I didn't know I possessed.

Because I was single, I had more time to devote to God. Volunteering at church regularly enhanced my leadership skills. As director of the radio ministry, something I never imagined doing, I interacted with business owners, did fundraising, and spoke on the air each week. Quickly my communication skills, discipline, and abilities to set healthy boundaries grew.

I learned to communicate effectively with people of all ages with respect and understanding. As I assumed additional duties, I was conscious of others who wanted to learn from me. God used me to help others discover their place while still discovering my own.

I used the years before I met my husband to reflect and learn about myself so I could prepare for the life I would have with the man God had intended for me. That time helped me understand the perils of tying my identity to something that wouldn't last. Singleness was my relationship status, not my identity. My identity is how I choose to define myself. Instead of seeing myself as a single person, I defined myself by my convictions, beliefs, and personality. Regardless of my unattached state, my foundational principles remained constant.

As promised, God proved he is with me even in what appears to be a dry season. What I thought was a nonproductive period became one of my most prosperous. What I planted in those years continues to produce a harvest. The leadership and communication skills I learned prepared me for my responsibilities as a wife, mother, pastor, author, and coach, and all the things I do today. The foundation was necessary.

Isaiah 43:18–19 reminds those in captivity of God's promise to free them. God would fulfill his promise. It wasn't what the people did that caused God to act, but his promise to them. Even though the trip back to Israel would be difficult, he would be with them. God's mercy is still available to us today, not because of anything we do, but because he is faithful to perform his Word. Prayers may go unanswered for a long time, but God is present. He often works behind the scenes, setting things in order.

God used that period of my life to teach me how to wait for his timing. Like the caterpillar, I was just beginning my process. The transformation of the caterpillar into a butterfly is a complex process, and each stage of development is vital. If something prematurely interrupts the metamorphosis, the caterpillar dies. Likewise, human metamorphosis is necessary for future development. Just as each stage of metamorphosis brings something new to the caterpillar, God was doing something unexpected, yet necessary in me.

I learned to be content with what disguised itself as an unfulfilling season. I moved from the stage of feeling like a failure to learning to enjoy the adventure. My mind and heart became open to God's plan instead of my own. When I did not receive what I asked for, I learned to be grateful for what I had. When I was single, I still desired to be a wife, but if my husband never came, I knew God had a good plan for my life. His ability to use me did not require marriage.

Now, years later, I once again considered my reflection in the mirror. I was single again but under different circumstances. I had enjoyed precious years as Scott's wife. Now I was a widow. Single again as a widow, could I reclaim the lessons I learned before I was married?

EXPECTATIONS

Unmet expectations can lead to intense disappointment. Disappointment causes frustration. Frustrations result from unmet expectations. What about when we pray and ask God for something? Believing God is listening, we pray with confidence and assurance. Sometimes it is tempting to become disheartened and discouraged in our relationship with God when he does not answer prayers and requests.

God's plan to encourage and restore hope rarely looks the way I think it should. Yet, even the most difficult of experiences provide life-improving lessons. The loss of a job may provide an opportunity to start a business. Financial struggles teach us to budget wisely. Whether chosen or forced, what looks like a distressing failure can provide a pivotal point. These changes may cause us stress, but pressure can strengthen and encourage creativity. We can develop better coping skills in times of heightened tension. Times of disappointment and failure can strengthen resolve. Many of the significant accomplishments I have were birthed after some mistakes. My most frustrating moments are where I have learned my most memorable and valuable lessons.

I did get married six years later. What a surprise when my long-awaited happily-ever-after wasn't only sunshine, laughter, and the complete fulfillment of my heart and soul. During what should have been a joyous time, I experienced disappointments. How often is a disappointment not rooted in the incident, but the result of expectation?

Life is full of surprises, rarely matching up with our hopes. Feeling like we have failed to create the life we desire or having unrealistic expectations are setups for frustration. Unfulfilled hopes and dreams in circumstances, events, jobs, and relationships can leave one feeling let down.

People sometimes disappoint us. We can become discouraged by those who do not behave in a pleasing manner. Individuals come into our lives and leave their mark. Some are with us for a short time, others for longer periods. The reasons our lives connect with others vary, but each one's presence is necessary.

While I have no power to alter others, neither should I burden them with unrealistic expectations. Everyone's level of expectancy is different. If I conjure up an idea or belief in my head and things don't manifest as I had hoped, I can choose to be heartbroken or not.

I realized that many times I expected something from others, but they were unaware of it, because I never communicated my desires to them. I felt let down when their reaction was the opposite of what I had hoped for. If I didn't communicate my wishes, it was unfair to hold others responsible for not fulfilling them.

When I experience disappointment and frustration, it is a signal that I've imposed expectations on how I think or feel others should be. And if I'm not careful, I find myself placing my expectations on God.

REFLECTION

Where in your life do you have expectations? Imagine surrendering all of your shoulds to God's perfect will for your life. How will believing what God says about you change the messages you tell yourself?

What do you think would happen if you communicated to those you are in a relationship with what you expect to receive from the relationship?

PRAYER

Dear Father,

As a young single woman, I wanted to be married. Now, I'm single because I'm a widow and my heart often longs to turn back the clock to the days when I shared life with the husband you gave me. Yet, you taught me you have a plan for my life. You have something special for me to do in each season, including this current season as a widow.

Help me yield to your voice, and act upon what I hear the Holy Spirit say. Thank you for inviting me to join you in building your kingdom. I pray for strength to continue and not give up in this season. I surrender all my cares and concerns to you, O God. In Jesus's name, Amen.

–CHAPTER 4–
TWO BECOME ONE

"Look, Evelyn, isn't that beautiful?" On the drive to see his church, he pointed out the birds in the sky and colorful flowers blooming in the field. He grew up in the mountains of New York; the smell of pine and the feel of fresh snow were integral parts of his childhood. Later, I found out how much of a staple the *Nature and History* channel would become in our home.

"This is my church." Scott parked in the empty, unfinished parking lot of the newly built First AME Church of Gaithersburg, Maryland. He served as a minister at the church, delivering sermons from the pulpit and teaching Sunday school lessons.

His face glowed with joy as he talked about the tenderness of his four- and five-year-old students. "The children's eyes light up when I teach them." Being a big kid himself, his smile brought warmth to my heart, and I knew he would be an incredible dad one day.

"We started the ministry in the auditorium of the local high school." He couldn't contain his enthusiasm as he showed me around the rooms. Everything was tidied and fresh.

Scott lived a short distance away and described jogging by the new building each morning. He recounted their accomplishments in such a short time and the wonder of watching the church grow.

I took in the beauty of the sanctuary. When I turned back to face him, Scott was on one knee. Knowing what was coming next, I quickly put my hands over my mouth to keep from shouting my joy. We were the only ones there, but somehow, it seemed inappropriate to yell during such an intimate moment in such a sacred place.

His eyes met mine. "Will you marry me?"

Without hesitation, I said yes.

This wasn't the first proposal he'd offered. After a month of conversations over the phone, he'd asked me to marry him. I had already said yes, despite having never met him in person.

But this moment felt special. We were in a tranquil sanctuary, our eyes locked in a gaze of love. The serene calm was enough to allay any fear. I believed God had brought us together, and I could feel the comfort of his guidance. I was about to embark on a season of joy and contentment. Yes, I knew many transitions lay ahead, but they were changes I had longed for, seasons I prayed would come my way.

Scott slowly placed the diamond on my finger; the cool metal felt like a whispered promise against my skin. The bright design of the ring he chose, without any input from me, was more beautiful than I could have wished for. I was speechless. Delicate baguettes glimmered, encircling the larger marquis diamond. The engagement ring was remarkable, unlike any I had seen before, and I had seen a lot of rings on the fingers of my friends when they became engaged.

I'm sure other brides-to-be felt the same, but I was certain my engagement ring looked especially exquisite with its glittering details. Not only did his choice of me as his wife display his good taste, but his eye for luxurious jewelry pieces was impeccable. This man was a keeper. The ring on my finger made our bond real. We had made a lifetime commitment to one another, and the ring meant we were officially engaged. This was what I had wished and prayed for. I had waited impatiently for this moment.

We set the date. In nine months, we would start a new chapter in our lives as newlyweds. With a desire to have the ceremony in my hometown of Lumberton, North Carolina, we began the daunting task of planning an out-of-state wedding. Our wedding felt like a destination wedding, even though we didn't use that term back then. Our guest list included family and friends from various locations who would converge in my hometown to witness our union.

Confirming the venue and deciding who would officiate were the first two items to check off my list, followed closely by premarital counseling. I had a pastor, he had a pastor, and my hometown church had a pastor. We selected and ordered the invitations. We coordinated our schedules. A few pre-wedding trips would be necessary. One by one, we went to work completing the details.

Our wedding day finally arrived. On June 1, 1991, the air conditioning hummed full blast attempting to keep everyone cool. I felt the stares of nearly three hundred witnesses in the church as the heavy, dark-brown wood double doors opened, and my brother gently gripped my arm. Martin was the oldest son, and he carried our father's name. I suddenly felt my arm shaking. I wasn't sure if the tremble was him or me.

Feeling flushed, I wished I could borrow one of the fancy fans I saw the ladies waving back and forth. *I'm not the only one who is hot.*

I silently prayed, "Please God, don't let me faint."

The ladies were in their prettiest dresses, and the men looked distinguished in suits and ties. Everyone was there for one reason. Their faces lit with happiness, and these invited guests came to celebrate our coming together as husband and wife.

My full-length white gown with long, puffed sleeves and layered undergarments added to the summer temperature. "I will not sweat," I told myself.

The sound of my heart thudding in my chest was replaced by the melodic notes of the music. So many questions swirled in my mind, but I felt peace knowing this was the answer to my prayers. Scott was everything I had asked God for in a husband. The enchantment of our new life filled me, even though I hadn't known he existed a year before.

Our marriage would be full of adventure and discovery. I had dreamed of this transition and invested countless hours of prayer into it. I would walk away from the career-focused life I had embraced as a single adult, carrying the weight of autonomy on my shoulders. All the knowledge gained during my season of singleness prepared me to be a wife. Now I had a partner to share stories and laughter with over meals. No more tables for one. No more coming home to the silence of an empty house after a long workday. At last, I had someone to converse with as well as to share my biggest ideas.

Anticipating the changes to come, I was eager to begin. Our pastor had offered wise counsel, and we had pored through helpful books and discussed marriage with other couples. We smiled at each other with assurance, and stepped forward, hand in hand, toward a fulfilling life together. Optimism filled the air, promising better things as the new season began.

Deeply in love, we were unwavering in our focus. Navigating this transition looked easy. Together, we planned a future in the suburbs with two incomes, two cars, two kids, and a comfortable savings account. Life wouldn't be difficult.

We both had faith in God. His strength would help us conquer any obstacle. Our parents were shining examples of longevity in marriage. With a place to call home, secure jobs, and no wedding debt weighing us down, I felt energy and excitement in each step toward our future identity as a married couple.

Ten months earlier, my nephew had introduced me to Scott. On leave from my nursing job in Washington, DC, I was living in North Carolina and assisting my mother while she cared for my father as he battled cancer. Initially, Scott and I spoke on the phone, feeling a spiritual connection when we prayed together. The foundation of our relationship was built on prayer and faith. We would be fine.

During our wedding ceremony, we vowed, "I will, until death parts us." At the words "in sickness and health, for richer or poorer," my heart raced. Having a front-row seat to my father's illness and watching my mother during those months made me acutely aware. Then the pastor added, "With the help of God, I will," and I felt my heartbeat slow as I repeated the words. Yes, with God's help, I could do anything.

The reality of living out those vows didn't sound hard. I was a skilled negotiator. I expected marriage would be like negotiating a wage-benefit package or a better deal in a purchase. Just keep talking until everyone agrees.

As we stood at the altar, fully ready to become husband and wife, my childhood family's pastor read from the Scripture:

"Love is patient and kind; love does not envy or boast; it is not arrogant or rude. It does not insist on its own way; it is not irritable or resentful; it does not rejoice at wrongdoing, but rejoices with the truth. Love bears all things, believes all things, hopes all things, endures all things. Love never ends" (1 Corinthians 13:4–8).

Love endures adversity and the challenges of life.

We vowed to put love first, even when perspectives clashed. No matter how loud our arguments became, we vowed to speak to one another with kindness. We wouldn't count accolades or track who performed their job, marital duties, or commitment to God better than the other. In our marriage, we would refuse to allow jealousy to rise. We promised to always celebrate one another. We barred rudeness from our home, in addition to blame, shame, and guilt. Most of all, there would be no condemnation for being authentic. I wanted to see my husband excel, and I knew he wished the same for me.

A marriage ordained by God requires we yield our desires to please each other. There was no room for selfishness. According to Scripture, we were now one flesh.

Genesis 2:21–24 says:

So the Lord God caused a deep sleep to fall upon the man, and while he slept took one of his ribs and closed up its place with flesh. And the rib that the Lord God had taken from the man he made into a woman and brought her to the man. Then the man said, "This at last is bone of my bones and flesh of my flesh; she shall be called Woman, because she was taken out of Man." Therefore a man shall leave his father and mother and hold fast to his wife, and they shall become one flesh.

God created Eve from Adam's rib. She would be perfect for him, but not identical. God announced the husband and wife are one flesh. While this speaks of sexual union, there is also a coming together of spiritual, mental, financial, and emotional harmony. Marriage is intended to be a permanent relationship, interrupted only by death. When death comes, we realize that relationship is also temporary. Yet, thoughts about the day death would separate Scott and me were the furthest things from my mind on our beautiful wedding day.

REFRAME

Scott and I had lived as independent, single adults before entering marriage. I'd made my own decisions without input, and so had he. Both powerful leaders in our respective fields, we soon learned we had to reframe our attitudes, perspectives, and expectations. Pleasure and satisfaction required finding common ground and compromises. While we shared the same goals, we held different ideas about how to get there. Synchronization did not come automatically for us. I quickly learned that even with God at the center of marriage, the adjustments were not as easy as expected. Had I rushed into something I was not ready for? Trying to mesh our personalities and live in harmony proved stressful. Every decision was a struggle until we concluded not everything was worth debating.

Coming into marriage with expectations, I fought hard to resist the temptation to be self-centered and insist on having things my way.

In their book *Building Your Mate's Self-Esteem*, Dennis and Barbara Rainey write that busyness is one obstacle to building strong friendships. They share how couples need friends who stand with them in difficult times.[1] Scott and I built busy lives that left little time for social interaction with other couples and friends. We were not intentional about balancing our time. These significant relationships meet needs different from the ones our spouse meets. We pledged to make our family a priority but failed to incorporate relationships with others. In moments of challenge, and when changes started to happen, we didn't have the support of another couple. My husband didn't have a close friend he could confide in, and as a result, I became his confidant.

As a young minister in the church, he needed someone to turn to. That person was me.

When he poured out his heart, I wasn't sure how to handle it. I'd never seen this side of ministry growing up. Did he want me to fix it? Or just listen?

I went through a significant realization and growth process in my role as a minister's wife. I wasn't the fixer, God was. Through prayer, I received guidance and valuable insight. Recognizing I couldn't provide the solutions or answers he needed showed a level of humility and faith. Interceding for my husband and praying not only supported him but also deepened my connection with God. My faith grew as I trusted God's plan.

I learned that being there for Scott didn't always mean I would have all the answers or solutions. Offering support, a listening ear, and prayers could be just as impactful, if not more so, in helping my husband navigate challenges in ministry. This was a beautiful way to strengthen our relationship.

But the struggles of life kept getting in the way. Marriage was like a puzzle, trying to fit both of our preferences into the same picture. I resisted as my individualism faded because I didn't want to change. My husband wasn't trying to change me; he was instead trying to understand and appreciate all my traits and qualities. When I opened my heart to how he expressed his love, I felt a deep desire to reciprocate.

We knew it was healthy to continue to engage in cherished hobbies. Preserving interests helps each individual stay true to self while merging into a couple. Scott valued his family deeply and wanted us to do everything together. My journey was one of discovery—full of sights, sounds, and new experiences. The adjusting, learning acceptance, and offering grace to each other was ongoing. During my first years of marriage, I learned that even in the most joyful times, transitions can be difficult.

SEPARATE YET TOGETHER

A healthy marriage consists of two people who foster personal growth while keeping a strong bond. This task can be challenging. Marriage is a journey of discovering the best version of yourself and encouraging and cheering on your spouse to do the same. While Scripture states husband and wife are one, this does not mean they lose their individual identities.

Mature people are comfortable in their skin and don't depend on the opinions of those around them. Confidence in their identity comes from being conscious of the purpose God has given them. This understanding makes it easier to move through differences of opinion in marriage without feeling threatened. Without a secure understanding of your identity in God, insecurities can arise. Validation from a spouse is important but does not define our identity.

Jesus said, "I am the vine; you are the branches. Whoever abides in me, and I in him, he it is that bears much fruit, for apart from me you can do nothing" (John 15:5). Scott and I discovered that to sustain a loving marriage, we must stay intertwined with each other and rely on the power of God. Keeping Christ in the center of everything we attempted to do was vital. We knew the effort would be great, yet we were determined to gain the skills necessary to adjust to the marriage.

Christ's relationship with his church is a portrait of a marriage. His presence is a constant throughout every stage of life. He is reliable and steadfast, showing up for love and conflict resolution alike. Regardless of where we find ourselves on that continuum, God's love is genuine.

To stay connected to God through Christ occurs through open dialogue with our heavenly Father. For our marriage relationship to grow, we had to communicate truthfully with each other. Learning to pray together about decisions that needed to be made generated goodwill and harmony in our home.

In some instances, I found it easier to communicate with girlfriends than my husband. I do believe men speak a different language than women, but I set out to learn his language. I was in that classroom until the day he left me.

Communication is important in every relationship. Some have developed the ability to communicate their needs effectively in certain relationships but not others. This action serves as a preventative measure to help people avoid potentially hurt feelings. If we are completely ignored when voicing our concerns, what then?

My marriage reflected my relationship with God. Through the years, Scott and I learned how to make each other smile with a simple gesture or phrase. My husband felt happy when we spent time together. Our heavenly Father is happy when we spend time with him. Being in a relationship with God doesn't take away from our identity. We are a more developed, stronger version of who he created us to be when in a relationship with him.

When we spent time together, my husband's face lit up with happiness. He wanted me to recognize and treasure the qualities that had made him take notice of me. When we spend time with our heavenly Father, we feel the warmth of his love. Nothing fills the heart and soul like a relationship with God. Through our connection with him, we gain a new understanding of our purpose in life.

In marriage, we set ourselves apart to be only for our spouses. A relationship with God requires we set ourselves apart for him. Sometimes it's difficult to welcome God into certain situations. I embraced Scott's love, and together we basked in the warmth of God's love, accepting each other's authentic selves. I received the purest of Scott's love when I rested in his words of assurance that he loved me just as I was and chose me to be his wife.

Similarly, the Word of God assures that God's great love is a gift. "For God so loved the world that he gave his only Son, that whoever believes in him should not perish but have eternal life" (John 3:16). Knowing we would mess up, God chose us and offered his love. A godly husband is an earthly picture of Christ's love.

Our belief strengthened our resolve to stay strong in the face of adversity. We both understood our life as husband and wife was part of a bigger plan set in motion by God. Uniting as one may present its challenges, but we believed with God's support, we could overcome them.

REFLECTION

What issues are you having difficulty with? What objectives are you working to accomplish on your own? Can you place your faith in God and allow him to guide you?

Some things will take a lifetime to accomplish but as long as you are moving in the right direction, keep moving. God is right there with you.

PRAYER

Dear Father,

Thank you for creating me in your image. You know everything there is to know about me; nothing is hidden from you. Psalm 139:2 says, "You know when I sit down and when I rise up; you discern my thoughts from afar." No one else knows me like you do. My weakness, my failure, and my idiosyncrasies—you know them all.

Help me love the mate you gave to me. Show me how to love in a way that my spouse feels loved. You created him too, and it's not my duty to try to change what you made. Increase our happiness as we come together intimately.

I can't expect my spouse to give me what he doesn't possess. No matter how much I love my spouse, there are desires only you can fill.

In moments of sacrifice, help me see the greater plan for marriage. In times of conflict, let me always turn back to the one who joined us together. Amen.

–CHAPTER 5–
PREPARE FOR TRANSITIONS

Around us echoed the sounds of laughter, complaints, and tears. Maneuvering the bustling campus, parents ignored No Parking signs. Everyone wanted to be as close as possible to their student's dormitory. Anything to shorten the distance between vehicles and the rooms where heavy boxes and furniture were being carried.

Back and forth, load after load, we helped our daughter arrange her things in the dorm room where she would live. Too soon, the car was empty. Our firstborn was leaving home for real. Could her childhood years have passed so quickly? Defining moments paraded through my memory, creating a cacophony of emotions. It's hard to believe that the time had come for us to settle our baby girl, who has grown up so fast, at college.

Where had the time gone? Wasn't it only yesterday when I had given a card to Scott and felt the glee of congratulating him?

"You are going to be a dad."

Scott made twenty phone calls that night to share the exciting news. I wanted to wait, but he was determined to tell everyone before the first trimester moved into the second. We were having a baby, news of unmistakable warmth.

Morning sickness began. Relief from perpetual nausea subsided only when I slept and finally ended when she entered the world.

Scott's mother stayed home to raise him, and he wanted to provide the same nurturing environment for our daughter. Two weeks before she was born, I said goodbye to my coworkers, knowing I would not return to the workplace.

Eighteen years passed like the blink of an eye, and suddenly, she was an adult. My enthusiasm for her bubbled up inside of me. She had worked diligently to get into college. In high school, she maintained her grades and studied for standardized tests. She took the initiative and filled out college admissions applications. When she got accepted into her first-choice school, we celebrated with claps and cheers. This new season of independence and responsibilities would be good for her.

Her dad saw this transition differently. While he supported her, our home was quieter—a reminder she was not there to share it. He remembered the little girl who ran to him with tears in her eyes when she needed empathy and reassurance. His mission was to keep her safe even while she lived away from the comfort of our home. We started sleeping with our cell phones by the bed. We didn't want to take any chances of missing a call from her.

In preparation for this transition, we did our utmost to teach her the life skills she needed. Moving forward, we would finally see if the lessons we instilled over nearly two decades had stayed with her. Would she remain true to the values we modeled, or would she forge an alternative path? Could we trust her to seek a place to worship near her college address? Would she heed our warnings about drugs and alcohol? What about our rule that boys were not allowed in her dorm room?

Our daughter had her dad's outgoing personality, and her growing social circle of friends was always welcomed in our home. We opened a world of adventure for her through travel. Daily we prayed for her safety and well-being. Now we watched and waited to see how she transitioned from childhood to young adulthood. We had faith that God would keep her in his guiding embrace.

I asked my daughter to reminisce on the lengthy path she had taken from four years of undergrad studies and two years of graduate school. "How was the experience of leaving your family home and starting college?"

She answered confidently. "It wasn't a hard transition because I was ready."

READY OR NOT

When we are ready, transitions are not as difficult. However, some transitions we can never prepare for. In Florida, hurricane season begins in June and continues until November. Months before, county officials offer the public a list of tips on hurricane preparedness. Many residents take heed and prepare a hurricane emergency kit including flashlights with working batteries, bottled water, nonperishable foods, medical items, a battery-powered radio, extra cash, and plywood to cover windows in the event of a storm.

Others do nothing.

Days before the impending storm, those who have not prepared appropriately hurry to do what others did weeks or months in advance. By this time, many stores have sold out of needed supplies. Heeding early warnings would save them from last-minute stress.

As the weather service predicts the path of a dangerous storm, authorities alert residents to evacuate to ensure their safety. On a beautiful day with not a single cloud in sight, why would I leave my house? Yet, preparedness requires the dispersing of large numbers of people to begin before the danger is imminent. Those who wait until the gathering clouds appear on the horizon find themselves part of a massive traffic jam stuck on the highway for hours.

Slow to heed the signs and warnings, some may never arrive at safer grounds and must ride out the winds and rain in unsafe places. As the hurricane draws near, county officials announce, "If you haven't left already, stay where you are."

Two times in the past twelve months, I've had to pack a bag and leave my home due to mandatory orders. The county issues evacuation with ample time, typically a day or two, to allow people to evacuate safely. I typically don't leave immediately, but early the next morning.

Even though we were both headed toward the same area to wait out the storm, someone dear to me left hours after I did. What took me three hours, took her twice as long. While she was delayed, traffic became increasingly congested. When expecting change, planning can be extremely beneficial to avoid potential frustrations.

Eighteen years is a short period to impart the life lessons we believed our daughter would need for the future. Training her included explaining concepts in language that resonated at a level where she understood instructions and consequences. Getting our precious daughter ready for the future helped her move confidently into her new role as an independent adult. The same preparation helped us to accept and adjust to living without her in the home and to welcome her natural transition into a beautiful grown woman.

PREPARING HIS CHILD

During the initial stages of my marriage, I was unaware the challenges I encountered would ultimately cultivate the resilience that sustains me as a widow. Our heavenly Father is intentional to use every trial we endure. Each one serves a purpose in preparing us for what lies ahead. As parents, we strive to equip our children for their futures.

God's Word instructs parents to be intentional about teaching their children. "And these words that I command you today shall be on your heart. You shall teach them diligently to your children, and shall talk of them when you sit in your house, and when you walk by the way, and when you lie down, and when you rise" (Deuteronomy 6:6–7). "The Hebrew phrase, 'You shall recite them to your children' literally means *repeat*. Parents are to rehearse the laws of God to their children. This command presumes teachers know their content, which in turn presumes concentrated effort and study. You shall talk about them is the practice of constantly repeating and reciting God's commands. It also involves committing them to memory so they become applied knowledge for life."[1]

My friends Philip and Karen are parents of three adult children. As full-time working parents, they started early teaching their children independence. They intentionally taught their kids how to live without them, ready for the real world. "When they were ten, everyone had to cut their food, pack their lunches, and do their laundry," Karen said. "We never looked at our jobs as raising kids, but our goal was to raise strong, independent adults."

As parents, we had a responsibility to prepare our daughter for her future. Others would come alongside to help us, teachers, family members, friends, and every experience she had good or bad, prepared her to live on her own. We are influenced by others and situations God weaves into our journey.

When my daughter said she was ready for college, I felt awe and admiration she had taken the steps to be prepared. Because of her preparedness, she felt confident she had the skills needed to live away from home. She knew how to do laundry, make meals, and think through decisions critically without parental input.

Now, she was ready to learn the lessons of being a college student, from the art of conflict resolution with a roommate to the careful management of the small sums of money her family supplied for her expenses. Sharing a dorm and bathroom, she had to get used to living in tight spaces and talking to people from different cultures—valuable knowledge she would carry throughout life.

Our chief aim, as her parents, was to ensure that our daughter was always safe. We wanted to help her develop independence. We were prepared to allow her to decide and manage her schedule. She learned to handle the frustration of not getting the grades she wanted and experiencing rejection from organizations she wanted to join. She realized her parents couldn't always give her what she wanted and sometimes she would have to accept no as an answer.

In the book *Boundaries: When to Say Yes, When to Say No, To Take Control of Your Life,* the authors discuss the fact that when parents lack limits, they may hurt their children's character development.[2]

We didn't want to rob our children of important learning opportunities. The task was challenging, but for certain decisions, we had to let them experience consequences and grow as a result. Without being exposed to change, children cannot develop the skills needed to deal with alterations, even minor ones.

Scott and I knew establishing boundaries was an important part of parenting. Boundaries were constantly shifting as our children aged. But age wasn't the sole criterion—the maturity of the child was also considered. Establishing boundaries can be a challenge, but the rewards of doing so are invaluable. Setting boundaries for our children had a tangible impact, which we witnessed firsthand. This experience provided our daughters with an opportunity to cultivate their inner strength and resilience.

As our first daughter transitioned into college, she gained brand-new independence and confidence. How would she react when confronted with so many enticing temptations? We clarified our expectations. Now she could determine what was the right thing to do. We reminded her of her worth and celebrated her unique identity. We knew that affirming our daughter's identity was crucial for her well-being and success. Would she stay true to the person she had declared herself to be now she was no longer in the safety of her own home? Would she turn her back on the life she knew for a different course?

This would be a moment that would shape her life and ours. We trusted God would protect her, and in doing so, our faith grew. We were confident the same God who had kept her safe up to that point would continue to do so. Her absence left a noticeable void in our daily routine. As we prayed for her more intentionally, we felt our prayer life becoming more meaningful.

No is a powerful word that can be difficult to accept, but that two-letter word is motivation to be innovative and investigate other opportunities. *No* not only taught our children, but *No* helps me consider the consequences of my desires and whether I truly want something. Often, I realize the situation was not beneficial, and thanks to God's no, I avoided potential harm. In the case of my husband's illness, I didn't always understand when God says no. Yet, I knew God is worthy of my trust. According to his Word, he has a great purpose in all he does, and he loves me.

WISDOM FOR THE JOURNEY

In the same way that Scott and I prepared our daughter for adulthood, God prepared Scott for his unique journey. He also prepared me for vital transitions. Some were difficult to accept, but I knew God would not leave me to deal with it alone. When I needed wisdom, I went to the Word of God and sought wise counsel from others. Life also has a way of teaching valuable lessons. James 1:5–6 says, "If any of you lacks wisdom, let him ask God, who gives generously to all without reproach, and it will be given him. But let him ask in faith, with no doubting, for the one who doubts is like a wave of the sea that is driven and tossed by the wind." As I study the Word of God, I am continuously learning how to apply spiritual truths to everything I experience.

Whether eighteen or eighty, age doesn't matter. Every day we live offers countless opportunities to acquire new knowledge and wisdom. Colleges that recognize the value of lifelong learning offer free classes to those over sixty, motivating seniors to keep their minds sharp and alert by learning new activities. Psychological scientist and lead researcher Denise Park of the University of Texas at Dallas and colleagues in a study involving 221 adults, ages sixty to ninety, found adults who were learning new skills showed improvements in memory over those who were not. Those in the study were asked to engage in a particular type of activity for fifteen hours a week over three months. At the end of three months, Park and her colleagues found that the adults who were productively engaged in learning new skills showed improvements in memory compared to those who engaged in social activities or nondemanding mental activities at home.[3]

I'm constantly yearning to discover something new. I feel immense gratitude for the invaluable lessons and knowledge I have gained throughout my life. Through problematic times, we can turn to God's Word for clarity and direction. Jesus said in Matthew 18:3, "Truly, I say to you, unless you turn and become like children, you will never enter the kingdom of heaven." Jesus used a child to teach adults a lesson about greatness. The quality Jesus points out about a child is humility. True greatness comes through childlike faith. Our daughter's heart was open, ready to take in the lessons we taught her. Our faith in God allowed us to trust that the results we needed would be provided.

How can we remain faithful to ourselves and to God when life throws us into turmoil? By following the teachings of the Bible, we can persevere through the tempests of life. God's Word provides a comforting reminder of faithful, unconditional love which leads us through each roadblock we encounter.

A good father carefully guides his children, teaching them the skills they need to succeed in all stages of life. Our heavenly Father gives us the guidance we need to be successful in life. The greatest teacher of all times endowed us with the Holy Spirit to show the way and instruct us in the truth.

Jesus said in John 16:13, "When the Spirit of truth comes, he will guide you into all the truth, for he will not speak on his own authority, but whatever he hears he will speak, and he will declare to you the things that are to come." Jesus had many things to teach his disciples, but he knew they couldn't handle them all. They weren't ready. But when the Spirit of truth came, he would assist and guide them. The Spirit of God continues to empower me to carry out whatever assignment he calls me to.

There are some life transitions we cannot prepare for. Even in those hurricanes of life, God invites us to pray, and in our prayers to boldly come before the throne of God and ask for wisdom to journey through successfully. Matthew 7:8–11 assures us this:

For everyone who asks receives, and the one who seeks finds, and to the one who knocks it will be opened. Or which one of you, if his son asks him for bread, will give him a stone? Or if he asks for a fish, will give him a serpent? If you then, who are evil, know how to give good gifts to your children, how much more will your Father who is in heaven give good things to those who ask him!

In hard times, I trusted that God would not give me anything that would harm me. Just as children repeatedly ask their parents for things, we can come to God in prayer.

REFLECTION

The constant in life is change and transition. Some transitions are dramatic—like the death of a spouse—while others are expected, such as an adult child leaving home to attend college. How has God prepared you for what you are currently experiencing? What have you learned and how can you use what you learned to help someone else?

PRAYER

Dear Father,

Remind me to look at transitional moments as opportunities. Let every experience, even those I prefer not to be on my life script, grow me into the person you designed me to be. Forgive me for the times I've sought to go my own way. Rather than rely on my strength, help me lean on you. Help me cultivate a heart of gratitude and acknowledge you in all my ways. Father, direct my path. Let my complaints be few and my thank you's be abundant. Help me see you instead of the difficulties. My times are in your hands, and I trust you to bring me to what you have in store for me. Help me to patiently wait for your timing because your timing is perfect. Amen.

–CHAPTER 6–
OVERCOME REGRET IN TRANSITION

Did I do enough?

The house was silent and still. After the funeral, family and friends said their goodbyes and returned to their daily routines. Alone with my doubts, I questioned if I had been the wife Scott needed. Could I have done anything differently to change his fate?

The reality of the relationship ending, after being his dedicated caretaker for so long, made me anxious and deeply sad. The nostalgia and grief associated with ending this vital relationship with my life's partner felt unbearable. Tears had streamed down my face as I hugged Scott's lifeless body for the last time and said a tearful goodbye.

When my relationship ended, my new story began. Ready or not, my life shifted. Waking in the morning my first thought was, *Scott is gone*. Lying down with the same thought each night became my routine. How would I deal with the regrets when there was no going back?

I constantly questioned if I had done enough for him. My rational thinking told me Scott had been ready to go home. He frequently spoke of going to heaven. Like a million needles piercing his skin, the pain had become more than he could bear.

Now memories of days gone by lingered. Disorientation overwhelmed me as I tried to adjust to this new life. My heart ached for the sound of his voice. Did I communicate my feelings to him clearly? Did he know how much I appreciated him?

The finality of my beloved relationship made me feel like a failure.

What If?

"It's Hodgkin's lymphoma," the doctor had said.

The words came as a shock to seventeen-year-old Scott. He had felt a lump in his neck, and after the examination, his pediatrician gave his parents the news. Scott would need months of radiation therapy.

But that didn't stop this determined teenager. After each round of therapy, he went to football practice. When he removed his uniform, the skin came off with the shoulder pads.

After five years, tests confirmed he was cancer-free. When we met, he'd been free of cancer for more than a decade. We celebrated the faithfulness of God. His medical history was a nonissue for me. Scott was a good man, and he was in good health.

But the cancer returned. Thirty years after his initial radiation therapy, the news shocked us both. For months he endured chemotherapy, followed by a stem-cell transplant that left his body weak and exhausted.

Two years after the transplant, fatigue and nerve pain led to the diagnosis of an autoimmune disease. The following years were a series of hospitalizations. We moved from crisis to crisis. In the end, he experienced a fatal heart attack.

In our effort to stay ahead of the autoimmune disease, had we been oblivious to something crucial?

During those rugged years, Scott initiated hard conversations, heavy with meaning. "I don't want to be kept alive through any extraordinary treatments. I don't want the girls to see me hooked up to all these machines in this hospital room."

He chose his resting place and carefully arranged his garments. "Please don't go overboard with expenses for my funeral. Use the money for your benefit."

We addressed the sadness that would come with saying goodbye. "Do you plan to sell the house or stay? If you leave this area, where will you go?"

He double-checked to make sure nothing had been overlooked. "No more tests." His voice sounded strained. "I'm exhausted."

Unable to bring myself to ask him to do something he didn't want to do, I agreed to follow his wishes. But what if the results were not what we had hoped for? I didn't want that responsibility.

In the final hours before the end, did I let down my husband by not advocating for one more treatment? As I reconsidered my decisions, I was filled with dread. Scott trusted my opinion. If I had uttered the words, "I want you to have the procedure," he would have listened.

Then our relationship as man and wife ended, and the finality of our bond crushed the breath from my lungs. Until death tore us apart, we'd held fast to our promise. We vowed to be there for each other in good times and bad. We had experienced everything best and worst, for richer and poorer, in health and in so much sickness.

When I looked back and realized what I could or should have done differently, regret washed in like a tsunami. I could have spent more time watching sports with Scott. I should have laughed more often at his witty jokes. Scott seemed content with what I offered and never asked for more. All he wanted, he said, was to love me. He was quick to apologize, making me ponder if he recognized the importance of an apology. He said "I love you" with ease and conviction.

And he asked, "Are you going to be okay after I'm gone?"

My response was always, "Yes. Life will be hard, but I will be okay." Part of my answer reflected the desire to relieve his worries. Deep down, I felt strong and confident that my faith would sustain me. I thought I was ready.

But I was not.

A powerful force, a survivor's regret, is impossible to ignore. The remorse and loss were too heavy to bear on my own. With my husband gone, how could I let go of my regrets and move into the new day?

NO REGRETS

While pondering my own regrets, I realized that many people deal with regrets. I spoke to my friend Mae who had experienced multiple divorces. Our conversation helped me draw some parallels between the feelings of a widow and the divorcee.

A beautiful woman in her fifties, Mae is single again.

When Mae and her husband grew too far apart, the fracture eventually led to the end of her second marriage. Both came into the marriage with expectations, bringing a unique set of ideas and feelings. After the divorce, she felt lost, and a fog of confusion and sadness weighed her down.

Overwhelmed, Mae found divorce to be a form of emotional and mental death. Gary Chapman in his book *The 5 Love Languages: The Secret to Love That Lasts* suggests that by learning their partner's love language, husbands and wives can ensure their emotional love tank stays full.[1]

Mae felt the love in her life draining away until her heart was an empty void. Her husband's love language was different, and he didn't know how to give her what she craved. When your love tank hits empty in a marriage, it's difficult to move forward. The reality of what is and the pain of what should have been crushes both parties, leaving behind a residue of sadness. The finality of a relationship may trigger feelings of failure. Mae felt increased despair when each of her marriages ended, like a heavy weight on her chest. Despite the initial appearance of a negative change, it can ultimately act as a catalyst for transformation in a person's life.

She is taking the time to truly appreciate her worth and self-confidence before connecting with someone else. This is of paramount significance. She recognized the importance of having mentors and being open to the counsel of experienced advisors. Mae frequently mentioned how thankful she was God placed people and resources in her life to help her.

Assuredly, certain relationships are of short duration; however, no relationship can remain permanent. Each significant encounter deposits something in our lives. Every meeting, no matter how short or long, can provide us with a wealth of valuable insights, even happenstance meetings. Seasons and circumstances bring change to relationships, and eventually even life-long connections are parted through death.

The connections we share are priceless. We were born to be social creatures, developing relationships through interaction. Social isolation can lead to emptiness and being overwhelmed by insecurities and fear. Research shows that no interaction with others can weaken a person's immune system, leading to diseases.[2]

The coronavirus pandemic, which swept the globe, resulted in many people being forced to go into isolation to prevent the spread of the virus. Many churches had to carry out their services virtually, and activity centers remained closed because of the imposed boundaries. The restrictions caused events to be canceled and families to be separated, which was unfortunate. Everyone felt some form of displacement. The yearning of grandparents to hold and meet their grandchildren was a common topic that kept coming up. For health reasons, the Centers for Disease Control recommended older people should not visit. Despite the strong desire to travel, a significant number of people made the conscious decision to avoid flying because of the fear of being exposed to the virus. For other reasons, driving was not a practical option for many.

Several years have passed since my husband died, and although I could cope well on my own, I still had the urge to seek in-person interaction after a few months of isolation during COVID. I grew tired of watching television and reading and craved something more engaging. I found that, while talking on the phone and video calls were helpful, they didn't fully fulfill my desire for deeper communication.

Compared to having a conversation in person, in our internet society, we typically communicate more frequently online. I am baffled by people revealing their secrets to the world on social media. With time, some relationships grow into friendships, but not everyone in our social media circle is a *friend*.

Social media allows me to reach people from my past and spread encouragement. While I have a close relationship with some, I'm keenly aware that the vast majority who follow me online are not people I know personally.

A friend is someone you can turn to for comfort and understanding, no matter how raw and vulnerable your thoughts may be. Friends trust one another to share their innermost thoughts and shortcomings without fear of criticism. Friends can have discussions even when they don't agree. A friend can be relied upon to protect our hearts and keep secrets safe. Human and imperfect, close relationships are founded on generous amounts of forgiveness and grace.

A loyal friend can lend a compassionate ear. They understand that sometimes silence is the best choice, and other times, an encouraging word makes all the difference.

Friends offer a helping hand, often at their own expense. Dependable, friends are around when life is going well and also during challenges.

"A friend loves at all times, and a brother is born for adversity," says Proverbs 17:17. "True friends and a true brother are there when you need them. How important it is to have some such close associates on whom you can rely when the calamities of life overtake you!"[3] Having shared magical moments with a cherished friend, I understand the importance of a supportive person who stands with me through difficult times. God positioned people in our lives to offer companionship, wise insights, and comfort in times of need.

Family members love us, but they may feel a sense of duty to be there for us. A friend may not feel the same pressure. I have been fortunate to have family and friends offer unwavering love and support. During the years of my husband's illness, many offered comfort as we waited late at night in the hospital. Some dropped off a warm meal or a good book, kindly offering to stay with my husband so I could go home and rest.

I learned to not quickly dismiss good friends but to recognize the value of that relationship. A loyal friend is someone to be treasured and never taken advantage of. I also learned some relationships are temporary, established to accomplish a particular result, such as a business partnership designed to conduct a joint venture. Business relationships may be fleeting, reaching out to colleagues to gain insight and support to advance in ministry and business.

A short-term connection occasionally grows into a more permanent relationship. However, striving to hold a temporary bond permanently can be discouraging unless the other person is searching for a long-term commitment. As the time approaches when our paths diverge, we often grapple to hold on, viewing the end of a relationship as a failure. Yet most relationships are seasonal. Few are long-term or lifetime connections. Some people are meant to be a part of our lives long term, while others come and go like the changing of the weather.

Relationships can be complicated and full of twists and turns. Even if we feel guilty for leaving the past behind and continuing onward, we can trust ourselves and our place in each period of our lives. Guilt is a lousy companion that keeps us attached to a situation that is no longer relevant. When negativity is the norm, a wise mentor or counselor helps us trade guilt-ridden thoughts for forward-looking, uplifting ones.

When I might have taken someone for granted, I take a moment to thank them for being a part of my life. When I have doubts about my role as a wife, I am reminded of the identity God gives me in his Word. Knowing he crafted me specifically for my husband's needs during his illness was comforting.

REGRET TO REINVENTION

Despite the regret she felt over the years she invested in marriages that ended in divorce, Mae found value in the lessons she learned.

The end of an important relationship is an impactful transition. Despite the initial appearance, a negative change can ultimately act as a catalyst for transformation:

Take the time to truly appreciate your worth and self-confidence before connecting with someone else. Recovery can take longer for some than others. Take what time is restorative.

Identify and mourn the loss.

Connect with mentors and be open to the counsel of experienced advisors. God provides us with people and resources to help us.

Consider what you learned about yourself in this experience.

UNDERSTAND YOUR EXPECTATIONS FOR THE FUTURE.

Most couples have the dream of a lifelong commitment when entering a marriage. As they embark on their journey of matrimony, they are filled with enthusiasm and optimism, looking forward to a future that they envision to be full of love, joy and shared experiences. Mae's eyes were distant as she shared the grand plans she had for her second marriage. "We envisioned a future where we would buy a home and fill it with the sounds of laughter and love."

Instead of sharing memories of growing old together, Mae's mind played a ceaseless stream of questions: "What mistake have I made? Did my efforts not measure up? Will I ever find someone who loves me for who I am?"

Divorce is sometimes even more devastating than the death of a spouse. The sting of rejection that can accompany divorce is not usually present when a spouse dies.

Toxic relationships can bring heartache but also provide invaluable life lessons. They offer wisdom on how to dodge future aches and failures. Examining our relationships gives a better understanding of our identity, recognizing what and who has a positive or negative impact on our lives. Achieving a sensation of satisfaction and accomplishment is what many people desire in life, believing those feelings show a life well lived.

I've discovered guilt can't be a motivating force for hanging on to a relationship that is no longer viable. In any relationship, I check my motives. If my intentions are righteous and I know I don't hold malice against anyone, then I practice the art of saying goodbye. People come into our lives with different motives. When the agenda has been accomplished, it's time to move into the next cycle. Many times, that means leaving an old relationship in the previous season. Not everyone is supposed to go with you into your new phase.

If we could only decipher the signs of impending disappointment, we could keep ourselves from ever being hurt. If a toxic relationship came labeled "do not touch," life would be easy. We can still gain knowledge from a connection where one person is acting out.

We teach ourselves to set boundaries, so we don't allow ourselves to be manipulated by others. Listening to our own needs and respecting the needs of others is necessary for balance. Unhealthy relationships can exist in any period of life, their toxicity lingering like a heavy fog.

Toxic relationships can develop anywhere, from the workplace to the church, your neighborhood, and even your own home. The thought of being rejected by a loved one can bring a chill to the bones, stopping us from speaking up. Although the relationship is far from perfect, the familiarity is comforting. Staying in a relationship for fear of losing that established connection is sad and deeply unfair to both parties.

Adjusting to life after the loss of an important relationship can be an emotional challenge. Disappointment over unmet expectations, grief, and regret are frequently complicated by frustration and financial strain. In the case of divorce, co-parenting while living in different homes can combine with the emotions of guilt and the heartbreak of children.

Yet, divorce and loss are a time of reinvention as people uncover the excitement of personal development and pursuing new interests. Apostle Paul writes in Philippians 3:12–14, "Not that I have already obtained this or am already perfect, but I press on to make it my own, because Christ Jesus made me his own. Brothers, I do not consider that I have made it my own. But one thing I do: forgetting what lies behind and straining forward to what lies ahead, I press on toward the goal for the prize of the upward call of God in Christ Jesus." Paul writes he has not yet achieved the fullness of maturity, but is striving to learn and grow, trusting God will guide him.

One widow friend shared with me her fresh start meant letting go of some relationships. She noticed some of her friends were no longer talking to her. There were no hard feelings on either side—their lives were simply moving in different directions.

I experienced something similar when I started to focus on my future. Some of my current interests differed from the interests of many of my married friends. They had been my tribe for so long I couldn't imagine life without them. Now, I was in a different season. How could I best navigate this change? I'm no longer half of a couple, but a complete individual. Those who have stayed are a support system, always ready to offer words of encouragement and a shoulder to lean on during times of transition.

Relationships, healthy and unhealthy, teach us about ourselves. "You can't change another person," Mae said. Her experience helped her understand the importance of balance to the survival of marriage, and the value of self-care in the form of doing what feeds her soul.

Like Mae, I realized I had to acknowledge my feelings, regardless of whether they were valid. I couldn't go back or rewrite our history. Scouring over my missteps convinced me I was so inadequate as a wife that I couldn't encourage someone else. Acknowledging the reality of the situation became my first step to letting go of regret. We are all fallible, yet God uses even our most embarrassing moments to bring hope to others. To guide me through, I trusted in God's divine mercy and abundant forgiveness.

Romans 8 reminds me I don't have to carry the guilt of the past. Paul starts verse one with the words "there is therefore now" which refers to Romans 7:25, "Thanks be to God through Jesus Christ our Lord!" God has delivered us through his Son,

Jesus Christ, and there is therefore no condemnation to those who are in Christ Jesus. This Scripture speaks of our salvation through the shed blood of Jesus Christ. The blood of Jesus covered every sin, mistake, and misstep that I did or ever will make.

Reflecting on past choices, I often experienced embarrassment, shame, and disquiet. But I couldn't live in that place. I trusted God and received grace.

Excessive guilt may cause a person to become depressed. Guilt that is constantly played over and over mentally can damage the individual and serve no productive purpose. But guilt is not always a bad thing. Feeling guilty is an appropriate response to wrongdoing, a reminder to acknowledge responsibility and apologize to those you have wronged. First John 1:9 says, "If we confess our sins, he is faithful and just to forgive us our sins and to cleanse us from all unrighteousness." God will forgive us, but restitution may also be necessary to make things right with those we have offended.

As we journey through life, our dreams and goals transform. I have a close friendship with a woman I have known since I was young. Over time, our relationship has changed dramatically. Despite the miles between us, we stayed connected through the warmth of our conversations. As life's tides changed, we adjusted our relationship to fit the changing times.

God remains steady in spite of changing circumstances, pivotal loss, and transitions. Scripture reveals the depths of who God is. His voice never leads us to a place of guilt and despair. Jesus said in John 10:14, "I am the good shepherd. I know my own and my own know me." Jesus laid down his life to be in a relationship with us.

John 10:27 says, "My sheep hear my voice, and I know them, and they follow me."

As I became more skilled in listening to God's voice through his Word, I found I was better equipped to navigate life's challenges and make decisions based on his guidance.

Releasing feelings of guilt helped me to be more thankful. Ephesians 5:19–20 states, "Addressing one another in psalms and hymns and spiritual songs, singing and making melody to the Lord with your heart, giving thanks always and for everything to God the Father in the name of our Lord Jesus Christ." When I chose to sing and be joyful, I saw my perspective change and my peace return.

REFLECTION

Regret can be a harsh instructor, yet it can also offer a powerful lesson. Redefining any regret as a teachable moment leads to fresh wisdom. What did you discover? How can you put your newfound knowledge to use? Regrets help identify our weaknesses and give us the chance to make improvements.

PRAYER

Dear Lord,

We experience broken, changed, and lost relationships within marriage, family, extended family, and community circles. With that comes great pain and suffering. Hearts are breaking. Thank you for being my source of comfort. You provide clarity, ideas, and creativity regarding mending relationships and recovery from loss.

My heart desires the day when wayward children reconcile with their families and are welcomed back home with open arms. May couples who have drifted apart be reunited in love and harmony. Your plan for me is beneficial. My heart is full of appreciation for the invaluable people and connections I have in my life. I thank you for the gift of Jesus, your only Son, who died for the sins of man and made redemption possible. Because of his death, everyone can find their way back to a relationship with the Father. Amen.

–CHAPTER 7–
TRANSITION TO MINISTRY

Our baby girl declared her independence. She crawled and got into everything within reach. I babyproofed the house, covered electrical outlets, and secured cabinet doors. Every moment she was awake required my full attention.

On this day, naptime was over, laundry was done, the house was clean, and the last item on my to-do list was to prepare dinner. I strapped my baby into her highchair, the only safe place for her while I fixed our meal.

Our eight-month-old daughter waved both arms and squealed her delight when Scott arrived home and came into the kitchen.

"It's time!" His excitement brought fresh energy.

I didn't have to ask what he meant. Scott was in school preparing for ministry when I met him. He was certain God had called him to pastor a church. He spent Saturday mornings on the streets, knocking on doors, talking to people, and inviting them to church.

Our current pastor knew the plan was for us to go out one day, and he gave his blessings. Transitioning from serving with leaders in an established ministry to working with pastors and leaders in a newly formed church was a huge undertaking. What would this transition mean for our young family? Certainly, there would be many additional responsibilities—were we ready?

Because my father was a pastor, devoted to the spiritual guidance of others, I understood the demands that would pull Scott away from family for extended periods. As a kid, I watched the depth of personal commitment required by my father to serve others. Growing up, members of our church were eager to have my parents share in the joyous and celebratory moments of their children. Such obligations assured a very busy schedule.

From watching my mother's life as the wife of a pastor, I knew something about the journey ahead of me. God wanted my husband to do this, and I would be beside him one hundred percent. Scott's introduction to church was mostly in his adulthood. Was he aware of the obligations and expectations of someone in a leadership role? People were sure to misuse his loving and generous personality. His strength was admirable, and I had to believe the same God who called him would remain by his side.

Our first church plant was in the hills of West Virginia. My husband still worked Monday through Friday, so his church-related meetings and outreach were held on the weekends or in the evenings. We met with local governmental and church officials for permission to use an empty church building. When all our efforts failed, we began holding services at a high school about forty-five minutes from our home.

On the first Sunday, family and friends came from everywhere to support us. The following Sunday, the crowds were smaller. Each week, the attendance dropped. There was no consistency, and only a few people returned for a second or third time. Outreach in the area proved fruitless. Discouraged, we wondered if we had made a mistake and stepped out in faith too soon. We prayed, asking God for direction. Should we close the doors to a church that wasn't growing? The answer came when Scott's job relocated our family to California. We closed the church and moved to the West Coast.

Our time in California helped us decide which direction we should pursue. While in California, we welcomed a second daughter, completing our family of four.

Scott's job ended early, and eleven months later, we returned to Maryland. This time, we opened the church in the community where we lived. Outreach proved fruitful, and the congregation grew faster than we expected.

Those early years as church planters with young children proved challenging. I wasn't much help to Scott on the front line, as the girls were my primary focus. My ministry role was mostly administrative. I attended meetings during the week in his place while he worked full-time to support our household.

During the week Scott worked hard at his job. His evenings and weekends were spent spreading the word about our new church. We didn't have any free time. After work most days, he went straight to an event. After church some Sundays, he would fly to other states to be available for Monday morning meetings for his day job.

A few months later, while the girls were still very young, I sensed God calling me to ministry. Reflecting on my role model, my mother, I was uncertain about how to respond to God's call. Because my mother took on more ministerial responsibilities when I was a teenager, I believed women couldn't pursue ministry until their children had gained a certain level of independence. I was reluctant to move forward when the Holy Spirit nudged me toward mentoring women. My husband was the preacher. Wasn't one of us enough, at least for now?

"You yourselves are our letter of recommendation, written on our hearts, to be known and read by all" (2 Corinthians 3:2). When Paul shared the gospel, the lives of others were changed. Those changed lives were the apostle's references, his endorsements.

The ages of my children would not interfere with what God called me to do. Whether I was the mom of toddlers, teens, or adult children didn't matter. If I continued to live my life in a relationship with God, I could set an example for others to emulate.

I began by teaching a women's Bible study in our home and eventually established a women's ministry at our church. Even then, God was preparing us for the future. Our time leading that church taught us humility. Ministry requires sacrifice and is not for the faint of heart. Most of all, we learned to lean heavily on God because apart from him, we could do nothing. That lesson came in handy many years later.

Those years of church planting expanded our faith in God and our love for people. Our dependence on God grew. When the financial burdens of the ministry became nearly unbearable, our reliance on God increased. When there was nothing else, we had to trust God.

Transitioning from a newly married couple to shepherding a congregation required commitment and solid work. Our life was a sharp reversal from the two people we were just a few years prior. We were still overachievers with high expectations, dreams, and ambitions, but we were no longer highly confident in our abilities. God had taught us dependency on Him. And we saw God meet the needs of the ministry and our family over and over again.

Though we gave much to those in our congregation, we gained more than those we helped. As the congregation matured, so did we. Our faith grew and we developed stamina. Yet, I sensed there was more to come.

VALUE IN EXPERIENCE

Our daughter continued to be energetic, boldly exploring her world. Her first toddling steps quickly grew into confident mobility as she gained experience and polished her skills. Her little sister wasn't far behind her. In the same way, Scott and I grew in our ability to care for the spiritual development of others.

Years later, we moved south and planted a new church—beginning from scratch. We had nothing in hand except a wealth of experience to draw upon, having done it before.

When we left Maryland, we intended to connect with a church where we could regularly attend services and become part of the congregation. However, God had a different plan in mind. This time, as we began planting a church, my confidence was less in my husband and myself and more rooted in God. Already he had shown me that many of my foundational beliefs—including those beliefs around which I could minister to others while being a mother to my young children—were rooted in assumptions about what I had experienced. I learned to commit everything to God in prayer and follow his lead. He continually broadened my experience, horizons, and my confidence in him.

We can display God's love to others through all stages of life. Every believer is called to be a beacon of hope in dark times, pointing people to Jesus. I want my daily life to be an example of godly living, the assurance that if I can make it through the tough stuff with God, others can also lean on his strength and trust his guidance.

My parents had provided role models for me as I watched them in church leadership. My own experience as the wife of a pastor was both similar to and different from my mother's role. For each transition in my life, I could draw from, build upon, and expand on previous experiences.

In the same way our daughters developed one skill after another, there was significance in all the things I went through. And all the things I went through helped me have empathy for others.

The spiritual and personal growth I received in these early years was preparation for the biggest adjustment to come. Too soon Scott would go home to heaven where he would be pain-free after years of deteriorating health. God would call me to lean on him in deeper ways than ever before. Helpers would come alongside to help me carry this transition and loss. I would learn to give to others even amid my pain.

Coming Alongside

God surrounds us with people to help carry the load. Trekking through the initial days of anguish, however demanding, I knew God would use what I was learning to prepare me to reach out to assist others who suffered a loss. That is what my life was always about, and this wouldn't be any different.

When my longtime friend's husband passed away seven months after Scott, I knew what she was feeling. I understood watching the numbers on the clock change hourly and not feeling sleepy. I could identify with the struggle she faced to remember simple conversations. The effort required to complete the simplest task was vast. Having to make all the telephone calls, repeating over and over, "My husband passed away." Even normal tasks like making a meal, washing the dishes, or cleaning the bathroom took extra energy.

My friend needed me. I didn't feel ready as a widow for only seven months. But I was the best person to help her. When I said to her, "I understand," she knew I was telling the truth. She'd been there for me in my husband's illness and passing. I'd been there for her during her husband's illness, and I couldn't abandon her now. I wanted a full year to seek some clarity regarding what my new status would look like, but that was not God's plan. Months after my loss, someone needed me. I needed to step forward to be of help to another grieving widow.

It was difficult, but God strengthened me to reach out and support her.

Every encounter we face in life becomes a lesson to be learned and shared with our community. Sometimes it's an individual, and other times it's many people, but whatever we endure is not just for us but to help someone else. I believe each individual has the responsibility to communicate to others what God has done for them.

Just as someone did for me, I could do for her to encourage her, reassuring her she would survive. I knew she would because I was still surviving. My journey was not complete. I had a long way to go, but showing up, I let her know there was life on the other side of the death of her spouse.

Instead of running away from my grief, I faced it head-on and refused to pass the time with meaningless activities. I vowed to pay attention to the pain and never hold back in expressing what I was feeling. This way, I knew I would learn how to help the next widow. I embraced the grief, allowing myself to cry and be sad, but not for long periods. I had every right to grieve; no one could judge me for mourning.

Grief is not only a feeling associated with death but can also encompass the pain of any type of loss. Gary Collins writes that

Grief is a normal response to loss of any significant person, object, or opportunity. Any loss can bring grief, including divorce, retirement from a job, amputation of a limb, the departure of a child to college or a pastor to some other church, moving from a friendly neighborhood, losing a home or other valued possessions, the death of a pet or plant, loss of a contest or athletic game, health failures, or even the loss of one's youthful appearance, confidence, or enthusiasm. Perhaps no two people grieve in the same way, and the methods of handling grief are unique and personal, but the pain of grieving is universal.[1]

Every person has dealt or will deal with grief. Any loss can heighten anxiety, and if not handled properly may impact one's health. I realized that if I didn't grieve the death of my husband, I wouldn't be able to move forward in a healthy way.

My friend and I grieved differently, but we forged a stronger connection through a shared experience of grief and loss. Our journeys were personal, but we learned to navigate our own way. Our friendship served as a source of comfort, understanding, and strength for both of us. We now have a deeper level of empathy for each other and for widows in general.

Grief is simply a sad response to missing something or someone who was once valuable to us. Sometimes we think our grief is the worst, but the pain is real to anyone who is having the experience.

Feeling the loss and searching for the lessons in the pain that I could use to help someone else was my new assignment. God can strengthen us to use the tragedies in our lives to encourage someone else, and that is what I needed Him to do for me.

REFLECTION

What have your life experiences and transitions taught you? Where is God calling you to give yourself, time, talents, and resources to bless and help others? What have you learned in the process that you can share?

PRAYER

"And I will give you shepherds after my own heart, who will feed you with knowledge and understanding," says Jeremiah 3:15.

Dear Lord,

Thank you for those pastors, leaders, counselors, and teachers you have called and placed in my life. Give them your wisdom and understanding to hear your voice clearly and follow close to you with joy. Give me love for my fellow sisters and brothers. Being in the community requires a lot of grace, wisdom, and patience. You equip me to be your hands, compassion, and companionship to those in my circle of influence. I have been positioned in this season for a specific purpose—to bring glory to you, my Father, as I serve my brothers and sisters in their time of need. Thank you for all the experiences that prepared me for life's transitions so I can be a blessing to someone else. Amen.

–CHAPTER 8–
TRUST THE TRANSITION PROCESS

As a caregiver, I felt the tension in the air, a constant reminder of how difficult life had become. Some days, the weight of the world pressed down on me. Our dreams and hopes for the future evaporated into nothingness. The life we lived was nothing we had expected.

For a decade, I prioritized my husband's well-being over my own, putting aside my plans. Scott and I dreamed of the day our children would be off to college. Despite the bittersweetness, we anticipated new adventures visiting unknown places. But I had been looking after Scott for four years by the time our youngest daughter moved into her dorm room.

When he received the cancer diagnosis, a wave of emotion washed over me, and my nursing instincts ignited. With years of experience caring for the sick, I knew exactly what to do. Over time, he required varying levels of emotional and physical attention. I'm positive I did more than needed.

Because the two of us spent most of our time together, our identities became intertwined. We spent most days at home. In the family room, we watched the news and chatted while the home care professionals came and went. Frequent doctor visits meant struggling to get dressed followed by a painful car ride. The sight of his face contorting and the sound of his groans with every bump in the road tore my heart apart.

"Go do something for yourself," Scott urged.

But it didn't feel right doing things without him. Why had God chosen not to heal him? I knew Scott wanted me to be happy, yet when opportunities came to do something we had talked about doing together, they were difficult for me to accept.

I reluctantly agreed to a few fun activities but didn't want him to feel left out. We were a couple. We should do things together. So, we did. We stayed home together.

Blocking out the need for interaction with others, I devoted my attention to Scott. It was my duty to care for him, and I concentrated on the tasks that had to be done. I kept medical appointments to stay on top of my health. Every Sunday morning, I attended church or watched the service from home. Scott and I bowed our heads together in morning devotions and shared communion as a symbol of our unity. However, I failed to realize I was pouring myself out to the point of depletion.

I neglected to nurture what made me feel good about myself, the person God designed me to be. The absence of a positive atmosphere led to an identity crisis. It was difficult to distinguish Scott's feelings from my own. As I fully embraced my role as a caregiver, something vital was missing.

During that difficult period, many people knew me as a caregiver, which was accurate but not the only part of my story. I am more than a title. I am a person with a story. My husband tried to get me to do more in ministry, and I could see the wisdom in this, yet I was swamped under the responsibilities I already carried. I love serving others. What better way to serve the Lord than to provide care to one of God's children? My husband.

Then, suddenly, he was gone. My husband met my emotional needs with affirmation. After so many years, I came to expect his support. His death meant the loss not only of his presence but his continual encouragement and the feeling of belonging. Once those things were absent, I understood how much I had depended on them.

The house was quiet, calls were scarce, and visits were few. After such a long illness and so many people helping over the years, I thought I had used up all my favors. Reluctant to express what I was feeling, I didn't want to impose any longer on family and friends.

"Why are you surprised he's gone after being sick for so long?" Several asked this obvious question, but I couldn't explain my feelings because I didn't fully comprehend them myself. Yes, my husband had an extended illness, but that didn't make my loss less real. Sure, he was no longer suffering, but my grief was not about him—it was about me.

Why did I suffer such a deep feeling of deficiency and vulnerability? The sound that woke me each morning was my heart beating. Yes, I was alive, but I was alone. He wasn't just in the hospital like so many times before. This was final. This was for life.

Previously a confident person, who was this woman staring back at me in the mirror? This was not the strong, independent woman people came to with their problems. This reflected person was emotional, losing control, an insecure shadow of who she'd once been. Whenever someone looked at me for more than a moment, the tears flowed. Who was this weepy woman? The sadness filled me with doubt and fear. Had Scott taken with him everything that made me resilient?

How does the new widow fill the empty days and lonely nights? How does a surviving spouse spend their holidays? The widows I knew seemed to function as if nothing had changed. I now know this was not the complete picture. They were pushing forward out of necessity, and I would have to do the same.

Weather the Transition

To weather the drastic shifts in our lives, Scott and I consciously looked to God to help us manage our expectations. Unable to change our circumstances, we found peace when we realized we had no power to modify anything. Our years of pastoring reminded us of the importance of sharing what we learned. Together, we composed a book for caretakers, reminding them of the significance of physical and emotional self-care.

Using our experiences to connect and help others, we focused on helping readers feel comfortable enough to ask for help. Speaking to caregiver support groups, our message emphasized the importance of being mindful and creative to preserve their identity even as they care for a loved one.

As a ministry leader and nurse, I have dealt with death on various levels. Some close up, others from afar. Each experience shaped me into the person I am today. Amid the chaos, I felt God's presence guide me toward my purpose. When life moved too quickly, I took a deep breath and trusted that God had me exactly where he wanted me.

Though we suffer in this life, in each transition there is an opportunity to trust that God is in charge of all. Through those years, I learned to rely on God like never before. I opened my heart to let him be my source of strength and hope. I had to lean on God's strength to survive.

I found absolute truth in God's Word.

When I thought the caretaking years were taking me from my destiny, I had the courage, the strength of character, and the unwavering belief to do what was required for me to take care of Scott. I consider those ten years to have been very productive. They were essential.

With each new day, as I faced my new responsibilities, I became more aware of the God who provides for our needs. Even with our rigid budget, my husband's pain medication often cost more than we could afford. Our two daughters were in different universities, both living in off-campus apartments. I'm in awe of how we sustained three households simultaneously. We gave faithfully to the Lord's work, trusting God would meet our needs. We were encouraged by Paul's writing to the Philippians in chapter 4 verse 19, "And my God will supply every need of yours according to his riches in glory in Christ Jesus." In our times of need, we witnessed the faithfulness of God over and over.

Whether a happy or difficult transition, believing in the God who made us gives us strength to rise above the hardships of life. For the believer, our faith in God is a comfort and a source of strength, knowing he will not let go, even in our darkest hour. "I give them eternal life, and they will never perish, and no one will snatch them out of my hand" (John 10:28). We do not need to worry, for God's grip is firm.

The difficulties I experienced during my husband's illness built an inner fortitude within, providing strength to persist in challenging times. God lovingly created us in his likeness, reflecting his divine nature. He gave his Son to atone for our sins and bring us back to our intended purpose. By studying the Scriptures carefully, we can get some insight into his identity, affirming who he created us to be.

CHALLENGES

In his book, *The 5 Love Languages*, Gary Chapman writes about the different ways people express love. He identifies words of affirmation, acts of service, receiving gifts, quality time, and physical touch as five ways people express their love. He explains that a "person whose love language is acts of service will do the things that your spouse wants you to do."[1]

When I'm showing love, I like to do things for others. Scott was known for his kind-hearted nature and his talent for giving gifts. I on the other hand received fulfillment when I served him. I attended to all his needs, from cooking his meals to running errands, driving him to appointments, and managing his business affairs. Those tasks were second nature to me. They translated into love. I invested the hours, put in the effort, and showed my support with my presence. It was simple for me to display love in the way I hoped for it to be shown to me. I tailored my plans to make sure I took care of his needs.

As a caregiver, I had a strong commitment to duty. As I became more aware, I understood not every wife behaves as I did. Some turned their backs and silently walked away. I had moments when I wanted to walk away, but I could not. I relinquished my ideas of what I wanted and realized God had chosen me before I ever knew Scott was in the picture. God entrusted me to be a source of comfort and strength to him during his illness. The sound of that truth ringing in my ears lessened my frustrations.

Learning to trust God during my years of providing care brought me peace and helped me develop new strategies for facing difficult circumstances. To survive, I needed to learn to distinguish between my feelings as a wife and my feelings as a caretaker. When my husband needed to release the stress of chronic pain, I listened attentively, taking my role as his main support person. I knew he was not mad at his wife; instead, he was feeling frustrated with the current predicament. It was necessary for me to remember that beneath the deep pain and frustration he was feeling, the kind and loving man I married was still there.

It was an ongoing challenge to confront what was so present. I was caught between the two worlds of my ministerial activities and the demands of my caregiving responsibilities. Scott pressed me to stay active in the church's ministry and serve those in need. The effort to keep my mind calm drained me of my emotional energy. On days when a swirling fog of exhaustion filled me, how could I reach out and help someone else?

Despite the harshness of winter, the promise of fruit in the spring is possible. Blossoming requires protection and warmth. The farmer carefully secures a blanket of cloth or plastic over the young buds, ensuring the trees stay warm.

God surrounded me like a fruit tree, protecting me in tough periods. "He shall cover thee with his feathers, and under his wings shalt thou trust: his truth shall be thy shield and buckler" (Psalm 91:4 KJV). He will *cover*; the Hebrew word used here, *sakak*, means to shut in, to block, overshadow, or make inaccessible, for protection.[2] *With his feathers* may refer to the larger flight feathers of a bird's wing. As for God's care, it combines the warm protectiveness of a parent bird.[3] In the same way a baby bird seeks security and protection under its mother's wings, I feel safe and secure in the protection that God provides me, as I am his child.

During my winter periods, the sound of others' gentle voices praying for me filled my heart with the reassurance I was not alone. Their prayers concealed and guarded me, helping me not to become too discouraged during my most fragile period.

For some, the pain of hard times lingers, leaving them unable to bounce back. The pain is so intense they keep it in their hearts as a reminder never to let anyone hurt them again. I have a genuine belief that we can move forward. It may take time and effort, but the reward is worth it. With a gentle hand, God guides and provides the resources to flourish.

The goal is to remain open to the changes that life brings, and not become too attached to any single event. When life falls into a rhythm, it's hard to break free and make a change.

Progress isn't always visible, but it doesn't mean things are not moving. Though a geographic move may not be an option, we can step away from the status quo in our minds. This requires immense courage to take steps toward personal growth. Negative settings are motivation to make positive changes.

You are fulfilling God's plans for your life according to his schedule. He knew you would be right where you are at this very moment at this set time. Change can be challenging, but when we relax and appreciate the beauty of the journey, we gain the most. This means letting go of the past.

REFLECTION

Are you in a challenging phase, straining to make sense of the disparity between your experience and God's truth about who you are? You may not have someone to tell you that you are enough. But you are watched over by a benevolent and caring God you can rely on.

You are where you are for a reason, and there is something valuable for you to find. As the days turn into nights, so do our lives and the events we experience. As we progress through each process, we can be satisfied with the knowledge we gained.

PRAYER

Dear Lord,

Even when it seems like the world is against me, help me put my faith in a divine God and not on my limited understanding of the situation. In this season, help me find redemption and a renewed awareness of hope. Provide strength for me to stay confident in times of hardship. Thank you for continually recognizing and embracing my worth regardless of circumstances. Help me have trust like Solomon who wrote in Proverbs 3:5-6, "Trust in the LORD with all your heart, and do not lean on your own understanding. In all your ways acknowledge him, and he will make straight your paths."

I cling to you in my greatest despair. I receive your peace for the disappointment of what could have been. I rely on you for the courage and strength to surmount any trial that comes. When I don't understand what you are doing, I can trust your plan. And in your time, all will be revealed. **Amen.**

–CHAPTER 9–
OVERCOME FEAR

In 1994, I felt a gentle tug from God to step into leadership of women's ministries. Immediately, fear sprang into my heart. With my lack of experience, who was I to fill a leadership role?

Are you sure, God? Me? I'm inexperienced and fearful. As I presented these honest and vulnerable thoughts to God in prayer, his Holy Spirit overwhelmed me.

Please help me let go of my fears. Holy Spirit, take the lead. As I took my concerns to him in prayer, I felt his presence with me every step of the way. All I had to do was trust him.

My heart aches when I remember the many opportunities I felt too fearful to pursue. What could I learn from my past? Rather than stay trapped in what lay behind, how could my fears be transformed into steppingstones toward a brighter future? I remembered the frequent times I struggled with defeat and didn't like that feeling. I could learn to respond differently to challenges and opportunities. Rather than add to those memories of feeling crushed, I would approach future scenarios rather than shrink back. With strength and courage from the Holy Spirit, I determined to become the person he called me to be despite the fear.

AFRAID OF SUCCESS

Surprisingly, I felt afraid of success. Why? Digging down, I realized my reasoning dictated that if I proved successful in a certain area, I would have to venture into uncharted waters. Facing the unfamiliar resulted in waves of anxiety, so I quickly retreated. I was an obstacle to my own success.

Once I realized and admitted my fear of success, I set a plan to partner with God to press through. Armed with God's Word, when fear crept in, I stood in front of the mirror and recited the promises of God to myself. These verses reminded me of his love. I put my trust in God, leaned on him as my guide, and purposefully believed he would steer me in the right direction.

Fear of failure looms in the minds of many. Even if our desired outcome does not happen, the Scriptures assure us God remains in control. Like Thomas Edison, we gain insight from our experiences. Edison's thousands of failed attempts to find the answer that would light the world provided important information about what worked and what didn't when he was inventing the lightbulb.

Daily and perpetual fear can lead to a deep sense of desolation. When I have allowed fear to hold me back, that fear turned into frustration and flashes of anger. The prescription for fear is trust in God, believing him to do what is best for us. You can take comfort in knowing God is aware of all the things that disturb you.

When we recognize the power of God's presence in our lives, we can be less anxious. From the beginning, God has ordained the foundations of our lives. It is only when we trust in ourselves that we should become apprehensive of the unknown.

Though I found myself resisting change, hindsight has shown change opens new, fresh, and almost always unexpected opportunities. Faith is the unwavering belief that propels us forward, even when the path is unclear. What makes it even more remarkable is God is the ultimate provider of the faith we require, and he generously bestows it upon us. Apostle Paul writes to his protégé in 2 Timothy 1:7, "For God gave us a spirit not of fear but of power and love and self-control."

"First and Second Timothy suggest Timothy may be somewhat timid and reluctant to continue in his role as minister of Christ. This reluctance concerns Paul enough to write to him and encourage him to continue and fulfill [his] ministry."[1] I could relate to feeling similarly as transitions and responsibilities came my way that I would not have written in my life's script.

Paul directed Timothy, and I could apply the same words to counter my natural excuses and fears by considering the great gift within—the Spirit of God. My perspective completely changed when I shifted my focus off my trepidation and instead looked fully to God.

David could face Goliath with courage because David saw how small the giant was compared to God. David's brothers compared the giant to themselves and noticed only their lack. My fears may remain in the face of life's challenges, but they no longer control me when I put my hope in the great God of the universe. To God, the object of my fear is laughably small. What a relief to align myself with God to face my challenges rather than tackle anything on my own. We can approach life's duties with boldness, knowing God gives strength, love, and the will to succeed.

God's love is incomparable and unconditional. In Matthew, we are given the two most important instructions from God: love God and love people with the same unmeasurable devotion. This kind of love is humanly unnatural. Yet, once again, the Spirit of God gives without limit the strength to do what would otherwise seem impossible. In my own power, so much is not possible. With God, all things are possible.

COMMON DENOMINATOR

Fear is a major factor in current society. Fear of catching the virus was widespread during the Covid-19 pandemic.

The media exploited our worries. As a registered nurse, I am conscientious when dealing with health concerns. Wisdom is actively taking precautions and then pushing aside fear.

Irrational fears can lead to confusion and becoming befuddled. Scripture outlines a healthy, orderly thought process. When fear threatens, we have the steps to put the situation into God's perspective. Paul writes in Philippians 4:8 (NIV), "Finally, brothers and sisters, whatever is true, whatever is noble, whatever is right, whatever is pure, whatever is lovely, whatever is admirable—if anything is excellent or praiseworthy—think about such things." Paul understood his thoughts could direct the course of his life.

Second Corinthians 10:5 reads, "We destroy arguments and every lofty opinion raised against the knowledge of God, and take every thought captive to obey Christ." Many of my fears stemmed from thoughts in my mind. What if I step out in this new area and don't get the support I need? My fears were not based in reality, only thoughts in my intellect. I needed to take these feelings captive because allowing fear, worry, and anxiety to run wild in my mind is the antithesis of faith and trust. Instead of being overwhelmed by fear and work, Paul formulated an inventory of morals to concentrate on.

True is that which corresponds to reality. Anxiety comes when false ideas and unreal circumstances occupy the mind instead of truth. Ultimately, thinking about the truth is thinking about Jesus, who is the truth (John 14:6; Ephesians 4:21).

Noble refers to lofty, majestic, awesome things that lift the mind above the world's dirt and scandal.

Right is that which is fair to all parties involved and fulfills all obligations and debts. Rather than quarrels and dissensions, think of the needs and rights of the other party.

Pure thinking leads away from sin and shame and toward God and worship.

Lovely refers to what attracts, pleases, and wins admiration and affection.

Admirable is something worthy of praise or approval and deserving of a good reputation.

Paul sums up this catalog of virtues in two words: excellent and praiseworthy.[2]

What is it about the unknown that causes us to dread change? When the change on the horizon promises a better future, many still feel apprehensive. Many times, fear paralyzes people, preventing them from taking advantage of great opportunities. Worry and doubt keep people stagnant, locked in their familiar environment.

Beginning fresh in an unfamiliar city, starting a job, or launching a ministry can evoke feelings of anxiety; *What made me think I could do this?* Facing life without my spouse felt akin to being paralyzed by the fear of the unknown as if the entire world had gone silent. Who would be my support when I needed a comforting embrace? Would I have to live the rest of my life without a companion to keep me company?

If I did not lean on God for help, strength, and support, fear threatened to drive me to worry unnecessarily about things that might never happen. Where I stood in life no longer worked and was no longer functional or life-giving, yet in those familiar walls and those typical routines, I knew what to expect. Even if the thing I worried about did occur, worrying about it was a severe waste of energy and would certainly not change anything.

Instead, I had to make a conscious choice to fill my mind with beneficial and encouraging words. God has given us the courage to confront our fears. "There is no fear in love, but perfect love casts out fear. For fear has to do with punishment, and whoever fears has not been perfected in love," says 1 John 4:18.

In *The Letters of John: An Introduction and Commentary,* John R. W. Stott writes that "love that spells confidence banishes fear. *There is no fear in love.* That is, there is no room for fear in love. The two are as incompatible as oil and water. We can love and reverence God simultaneously, but we cannot approach him in love and hide from him in fear at the same time"[3] (emphasis added).

The answer to fear is love, the only force more powerful. Fearful persons, out of love for God and neighbor, may do what they otherwise would fear to do. Perfecting it comes about by following Christ's Word rather than one's feelings of fear.[4]

It's quite common for humans to experience dread when changes occur. A variety of factors can cause it, ranging from a fear of the unknown to a reluctance to step outside of our comfort zones. Understanding the reasons behind our fear of change is essential for successfully navigating it. We must ensure we gather all the information by digging deep and leaving no detail unexplored.

The realization that I'd be approaching retirement years alone, like so many other widows, hit me hard. Would it be possible for me to thrive, rather than just survive, alone? The need for human connection is hard-wired into our very being, a reflection of God's design for us to be in relationships. The Creator acknowledged the importance of companionship by creating Eve for Adam, yet I found myself without a companion.

God's perfect love disperses fear. When fear creeps in, I imagine the warmth of God's embrace and the sound of his comforting voice. He's always hovering, like a protective parent, never letting me out of his sight. During those contemplative moments, I always feel God reassuring me. Each day, I receive the reminders I need to stay focused and motivated.

Fear may whisper you are inferior and not competent enough. It's important to recognize these thoughts and feelings are not necessarily accurate reflections of your worth or abilities. Our strengths and weaknesses are unique to each of us, and it's natural to experience self-doubt from time to time. Overcoming these feelings and developing a positive self-image takes time, self-awareness, and self-compassion. While change may terrify some, others may find it exciting and thrive in unfamiliar circumstances.

God gave us the qualifications we needed to succeed before he asked us to join him in the mission. Fear of change can be managed and overcome with the right mindset, support, and strategies. God put people in my path who would offer me guidance and support anytime I felt fear sneaking in. I learned not to be shy about seeking advice if I needed help from mentors, coaches, counselors, or friends—I learned to ask. In some cases, there were things I needed to learn, so I enrolled in available courses. Knowledge can help demystify and reduce fear.

Deep-breathing exercises proved helpful for me, but most of all spending time in God's Word. This reaffirmed his great love for me and that I didn't have to live in fear of my future. God already had it all planned out, and all I needed to do was to trust him.

REFLECTION

What experience has brought fear and insecurity into your life? Rejection? Loss?

What standards do you believe you have to measure up to?

Where is God inviting you to take a leap of faith? Is fear whispering in your ear that you're not able? You may feel overwhelmed, but remember God partners with you, so what he has asked of you will come to fruition. Start your day with prayer, asking God for guidance and strength.

Prayer

Dear Lord,

Fear and anxiety overwhelm me. Your Word tells me not to be afraid, but this insecurity seems to always find a way in. With so many concerns, it's hard not to be anxious. But God I ask you to wrap your arms around me and anyone who is afraid. Remind me I can lean on you and you alone hold the future. You are worthy of my trust.

Let me find comfort in your Word and assurances in your promises. Heavenly Father, help me get through the days without worry and fear but with power, love, and a sound mind. As Paul writes in Philippians 4:6 "Do not be anxious about anything, but in everything by prayer and supplication with thanksgiving let your requests be made known to God." I bring my fear to you and ask you to bolster my heart with faith and trust in you. Thank you for your help. Amen.

–CHAPTER 10–
FIND FREEDOM

Since sixth grade, I'd always harbored a deep-seated dream: I wanted to be a nurse. Despite having no medical background in my family, my desire to be a nurse grew stronger with age. I excelled in science and biology classes, absorbing knowledge like a sponge. My teachers noticed my unwavering commitment and encouraged me to pursue my dreams. My parents, too, provided unwavering support, knowing that their daughter's dream was more than a fleeting aspiration.

Upon graduating from high school, I eagerly enrolled in a nursing program at the local college. My journey through nursing school was challenging but deeply rewarding. I spent countless hours studying anatomy, learning medical procedures, and practicing bedside care on mannequins. However, my enthusiasm waned when math for nurses presented a challenge. The concepts of drams, millimeters, and calculating medication doses were difficult for me to grasp. Despite my proficiency in math, this was a completely new and foreign idea to me. No matter how much I stayed after classes and gave it my all, I still wasn't succeeding. It seemed like my dream was slipping away, but then everything fell into place, and I knew what to do.

During my clinical rotations at the nearby hospital, my compassion and dedication shone brightly. Patients and families frequently remarked on my caring personality and warm smile. I tried to treat each person I encountered with the utmost respect and empathy, making them feel seen and heard during their time of vulnerability.

Finally, my dream became a reality. I passed my nursing exams and earned a nursing license. The expectation was if I graduated from that school, I would have a job waiting at that hospital. I didn't consider the possibility of any other medical facilities. My restricted view at the time made me believe I'd be stuck in that place forever.

The feeling of accomplishment was palpable as I received my first assignment at the local hospital on graduation day. While I didn't get the position I wanted, they assured me they would reassign me as soon as an opening became available. I was content with the familiarity of continuing to live at home and the absence of pressure from my parents to move out.

Two years later, both my younger sisters were attending college, while I was an adult still living with my parents.

My dreams and aspirations began to tug at my heart, urging me to spread my wings and explore the world beyond my childhood home. One sunny afternoon, I decided it was time to have a conversation with my mother. I had been contemplating this moment for weeks, rehearsing the words in my mind, and now, with a deep breath, I walked outside where my mother was sitting on the porch. She looked up. "What's on your mind?"

"I feel it is time for me to move into my own place."

Surprise flashed in her eyes. Processing my words, she blinked a few times. "I had grown so comfortable with you being here, I thought you would remain with me forever." She paused. "Of course, I knew you would leave at some point, but I just didn't want to face it."

I reassured my mother the apartment I was looking at wasn't far away. "That doesn't make it any easier for me, but I always knew the day would come."

My new apartment was within walking distance from work. With this big move came a rush of liberty and the delight of embracing new horizons. I learned to budget, deal with people on a professional level, and haggle for the furniture I wanted to buy.

My new home was more than just a living space—it meant something more. A representation of my dreams becoming a reality, it motivated me to create the life I envisioned. A beautiful chapter was beginning in my life, filled with adventure, challenges, and newfound freedom.

THIS MOTHER'S STORY

Having experienced motherhood for myself, I understood my mother's wish for me to not move out. Two years had passed since our eldest daughter started college, and now it was our youngest daughter's turn. Watching her depart for the university campus left me feeling empty, a reminder of our new status as empty nesters.

To ensure our children were well-rounded, Scott and I delayed pursuing our dreams. Our children were a top priority, and we wanted to ensure they had a broad range of experiences. Most of our activities revolved around them.

With the house no longer filled with children, a peaceful quiet overtook our rooms. No more organizing carpools, packing lunches, or planning for sleepovers. How do parents keep themselves busy with the extra time they have?

My home quieter with the children gone, evoked a variety of responses. Many factors can influence how a family handles this transition, including how many children have already left and what emotions swirled around the household as the last one prepared to depart. I knew adjusting to this new chapter would be complicated if I tried to hold on when it was time to let go.

An empty nest was an opportunity for Scott and me to reconnect. We could outline new objectives as a couple or simply carve out deserved personal time. I wondered how isolating the experience might feel for some single parents or perhaps the transition felt like a source of liberation.

After twenty years, our house was quiet, lacking the exuberant energy that only kids bring. How would I spend the extra time with more hours in the day? I soon realized we quickly filled those hours with other obligations.

Once the kids were out of the house, Scott and I could concentrate on ourselves again. I felt satisfied with what we had achieved, and my heart pulsated with enthusiasm for what was to come. Though my husband was ill, we hoped he would recover. In the meantime, we were determined to find activities he could manage with his existing energy.

We no longer had to plan our time around our children's needs and activities. We would slow our pace, spending Saturdays listening to the waves crash on the beach instead of being on the sidelines at the soccer field. With the kids out of the house, I took down the calendar from the refrigerator door. With no concerns about when the school opened or which days the campus would be closed, I felt free from school schedules and free from the district calendar.

At the gym, I heard someone inquire, "Wasn't today the first day of school?"

I smiled, shook my head in uncertainty, and kept going with my exercise.

Jill Savage writes in her book, *Empty Nest, Full Life: Discovering God's Best for Your Next,* about the light-bulb moment when she and her husband Mark realized they could travel together. "You've worked hard for your freedom, now is the time to enjoy it."[1]

PREP FOR THE EMPTY NEST

After many years of neglecting date nights to stay connected, parents can suddenly realize they have few shared interests. With days consumed by parenting issues, their marriage has been neglected, and time for meaningful connection has been scarce. By carving out time for the two of them, parents may find it easier to adjust when their children leave the nest.

Keeping my self-worth as my children grew and left home gave me a foundation to rely on during times of unsteadiness. Knowing our own identity helps when it's time to shift between the phases of life. Remembering every season has a purpose makes navigating change easier. Constantly reevaluating who we are is frustrating. Having a purpose takes a distinctive shape in each stage of life.

As empty nesters, my husband and I transitioned into a new season with a revitalized ambition, an array of ideas, and a newly established identity. Still very parental, we gained additional responsibilities that changed the dynamic. Parents strive to teach children lessons through their actions rather than formal instruction. Growing up, I recall sitting at my mother's feet while she read devotions. Yet even after I became an adult, she taught me through her words and actions.

WHO I AM NOW

I fondly remember the bright white walls of my grandmother's two-story house, where I spent my childhood. Just off the dining room, the creaky stairs leading to the second floor beckoned. I think there were about twenty wooden stairs that creaked with every step. We hopped up the stairs two at a time to reach the second floor where the kids slept faster. Despite our efforts to get there quickly, skipping steps only delayed our arrival.

Life is like climbing a staircase; skipping steps won't necessarily get you to the top faster. That kind of thinking may lead to repeating the same mistakes over and over. To avoid slipping and having to begin over again, slowly and cautiously climb the stairs one step at a time. When we raced up the stairs, I felt the heat of exertion radiate off my skin. But the person who took the climb one step at a time usually arrived at the top first.

The journey brings appreciation for the results. The lessons learned in the process are invaluable. When I feel most helpless is when I learn the most. Each experience validates the importance of appreciation, patience, and self-awareness.

Greatness has a price attached. Influential leaders commonly report they took many small steps to reach the heights of success they've achieved. The process requires focus and attention to detail. Despite criticisms, they refused to quit trying.

Finding oneself again after a notable transition can be intimidating and full of emotional highs and lows. Life changes quickly, and today's reality may not be the same as tomorrow's. Despite incredible odds, would I act as if the situation would stay the same forever? Familiarity propagates comfort and contentment. To become the best version of myself is to step into the unfamiliar. Like growing pains, this feels achy and uncomfortable but is necessary. Even something difficult and stressful can prove beneficial.

Every new season, including this one, provided something new to explore. Aging allows an opportunity to gain wisdom, the familiar feeling of taking a deep breath and letting oneself experience everyday wonders. Listening to others and learning from books gave me knowledge, but life also forced me into places I never wanted to go. The wisdom I gained from the past equipped me for future experiences. The new season brought an opportunity to highlight my tenacity in a different light.

WATCH WHAT YOU SAY

The Bible teaches that "Death and life are in the power of the tongue, and those who love it will eat its fruits" (Proverbs

18:21). Words are described as being as powerful as a sword. The words that come from our mouths are like a feast for our souls, or we can talk ourselves out of success through the negative things we tell ourselves. Refer to yourself with a certain name frequently enough and you are likely to believe the label. Because it takes equal effort to pronounce the word *winner* and the word *loser*, we can empower ourselves by using positive words and phrases.

Words people say and words we believe about ourselves can influence identity. There is potency in our self-talk to influence our lives positively or negatively. Our physical appearance can impact our identity. If we don't like the way we look, it impacts how we feel and what we say about ourselves. When the color of my lipstick is wrong, I can hear a voice in my head telling me it's not the right shade. The best course of action is to take it off, so I don't continue negative self-talk for the rest of the day.

People are two distinct entities—what you do and who you are. I spent many years as a clinical nurse and cherished the ability to make a difference. When our first daughter was born, I stayed home and devoted my time to her instead of continuing my clinical nursing career. My family became my top priority, and I was determined to steward my assignment well. My choice brought my career advancement to a standstill. I worked tirelessly to ensure our home felt like a secure and nurturing space where our family could grow and flourish.

One day in a restaurant during a family vacation, I saw an elderly gentleman collapse and start shaking.

"Evelyn," my brother said, "can you help him?"

I thought he meant to pray. At that moment, I didn't remember I was a nurse. I hadn't practiced for a while, and a lot had changed. Declaring my profession as a nurse filled me with apprehension. Did I still possess the capabilities?

I don't know when it happened, but I had ceased defining myself as a nurse. This encounter prompted a reconsideration of the notion that identity is linked to one's profession rather than one's essence. That day in the restaurant, it could have been tempting to resort to using self-deprecating language. However, I came to understand that my worth didn't hinge on the nursing skills I possessed; instead, my identity is rooted in God's opinion of me. To understand God's perspective is to rework the language I use. Constantly undermining success can become a way of life. When thoughts move away from the Bible and toward circumstances, negative chatter takes over.

The hurt of a verbal attack can leave lasting pain far greater than physical pain. Even when not immediately apparent, the negative words can wear down our determination. Some medical statistics prove that having a positive attitude helps the body heal quicker.

Even when faced with an incurable illness, patients can benefit from having positive people around them. I witnessed this frequently with my husband—when close friends visited, his entire mood would transform. The laughter and the energy his friends brought proved to be as therapeutic as his pain medication.

That is also a key factor in my strong belief in praying for healing, regardless of the severity of the illness. While I understand not everyone may experience physical recovery, prayer instills hope. I prefer embracing a mindset rooted in faith when confronted with death rather than succumbing to hopelessness.

A study of people over the age of fifty reported, "Those who had more positive thoughts about aging lived longer."[2]

Applying this optimistic mindset can extend to various facets of life. Employing positive language to affirm our identity in each season of life can profoundly influence our self-perception. Once our children were grown and out of the house, and our life was quieter, we remembered our worth as God's creation. As parents, we dedicated ourselves to working diligently to provide a loving home for our daughters. Most parents labor tirelessly to ensure children have a life of prosperity with all the resources they need to thrive.

We knew we could look at this empty-nest transition as a period of solemnity or a period of uncovering new possibilities. Planting our identity in a fleeting moment of life leads to complications when anything shifts from our expectations. Could it be the experience was simply meant to teach us, and we failed to appreciate the lessons we were meant to learn?

Establishing an identity for the first time can be a daunting challenge. Having to redefine and reimagine it with each passing season is emotionally draining. Identity is embedded in values, beliefs, and experiences. A *Psychology Today* article states that "identity relates to our basic values that dictate the choices we make. These choices reflect who we are and what we value." The author continued that a person can hold multiple identities at the same time. "Identity is never *final* and continues to develop through the lifespan."[3]

Becoming empty nesters can have a profound effect on our identity as we redefine our role in life. Though our efforts shift and develop, despite the changes, our core identity remains constant. Many beliefs and values our parents taught speak to the core of who we become. Concentrating on the distinctiveness of each phase of life, we progress more smoothly when the time comes. In those early years with small children, the day-to-day monotony felt overwhelming with the sound of crying and the smell of diapers in the air. Will they ever mature and take responsibility? Time stood still. The sleepless nights and never-ending needs of a newborn were hard to handle, but the eighteen years passed by in a flash.

Most parents of grown-up children concur that childhood for their offspring flew by in an instant. We want to offer so much wisdom in the short years they are young and at home, but some lessons our children must discover for themselves. Disappointments remind children to stay humble. Learning to go without can lead to a grateful heart. Delays can be maddening, leaving one feeling frustrated and overwhelmed. But that is how patience is developed.

Cherish the moments and be supportive of those who are still raising children. If you are empty nesters, you can invest in your grandchildren, nieces, nephews, or other people's children to feel the joy of raising kids again. Young people seek the authenticity of relationships they can feel and touch.

When their last child left home, Philip and Karen were already in the mode of having their own time as a couple. They enjoyed travel and embraced the opportunity to show their children the world through their eyes. Taking their time and living within their means, they journeyed across the United States twice in their camper, each trip lasting six weeks.

Preparing their children for the future, they instilled independence from an early age, teaching them how to thrive. The older their children grew, the less they enjoyed the camping trips. They wanted to fly and get to places quickly. My friends were smart. "Our children were passionate about sports, and we shared their enthusiasm as we traveled with them to their competitions."

The cost of hiring a sitter to stay with three children was costly, so Philip and Karen found activities they could share as a family. They felt strongly that parents should never completely abandon their hobbies for their kids. To adjust well to the various seasons, they enjoyed each other's company, engaging in activities that brought them closer even while raising children.

SMALL CHANGES

Life gives us moments to teach our children the skills they need to become independent. Parents help children move forward into the next stage of their lives, be it college, the military, or the workforce. As they progress up the ladder of life, they will have special memories like the time they nervously said goodbye on the first day of preschool and the laughter and stories that came from the adventures at summer camp.

What valuable lessons does a child absorb from these moments of growth? Preschool usually provides a safe and nurturing environment that allows children to practice trust. They learn parents return at the end of the school day. This helps children understand that when people make a promise, they will keep it. The child experiences routine, practices ways to cooperate with others, and develops communication skills. Witnessing other children who are in pain or distress, children develop empathy. They learn to show respect for adults, particularly their teachers. At preschool, the teacher helps cement lessons the parents teach at home, such as placing toys back in their rightful place when playtime is done.

While I believe children should go home when it's time for sleep, I've seen that sleepovers offer children the chance to try new foods and adjust to different circumstances. They brush their teeth, put on pajamas, and slip under the covers without relying on Mom and Dad. Allowing my child to grow independently helps ease feelings of separation anxiety. Being away from home overnight can be an intimidating concept for some children. The first time a child goes to a sleepover, parents may feel a knot in their stomach from the worry.

Age-appropriate summer camps provide children with a chance to mingle and make friends outside their immediate family. As a child interacts with people from different backgrounds and cultures, they gain an understanding of social advocacy and communication techniques. Parents hone their due diligence as they examine any program or place they are thinking of sending their children to, even if it's the home of a relative or close friend.

My husband and I took great care to ensure we equipped our daughters with the skills needed for the future, though we were inclined to do too much for our children, tasks they could fully do themselves. We committed to helping our kids if they stumbled. Some would call us lawnmower parents, as we intervened, trying to mow down obstacles that would prevent them from success. Our goal was to sustain a harmonious equilibrium.

We paid more attention to their lives and activities than was probably necessary. In hindsight, we could have provided additional opportunities for adventure when they were young. How much liberty should a parent give their child? It's a hard question to answer, and my husband and I wished to prevent our children from needless suffering.

As the type of person who errs on the side of caution, my struggle is making sure I don't pass my worries to my kids. My intent to protect them can be greater than my desire to let them grow and learn. One day, our daughter telephoned feeling disheartened. We had talked about the issue beforehand, and she could have avoided frustration by heeding my advice. Yet, life taught her about actions and responses because she didn't listen to wise advice.

A *USA Today* article asked, "How do you tell the difference between legitimate helping or even a necessary parent rescue versus lawnmower parenting?"[4] Each child is unique, and each request needs to be evaluated before deciding to step in or to let them figure it out.

A staff member at my daughter's middle school called. We were neighbors, and I was grateful she kept an eye on my child. She had asked why my daughter was not eating and learned someone had stolen her lunch. When my neighbor offered to buy lunch for my daughter, she declined. "I'm concerned she is skipping her meal," my neighbor said.

Every situation has positives and negatives. My kids forgot school assignments and left their books for class at home. Sometimes, I'd deliver the forgotten items, and other times, I didn't, depending on which child and how often she forgot. If I continually reminded them and they still forgot, the consequences became a lasting lesson. Each incident provided a chance to consider whether the knowledge gained was more beneficial than the consequence of forgetting the item. Would this moment help them develop valuable life skills? That day, I drove to school, bringing my daughter a replacement lunch.

Developing an understanding of oneself helps a teen develop strong self-esteem and a solid identity. Dating can strengthen the communication and interpersonal skills needed to maintain a healthy relationship as successful adults.

Going on a date for the first time can make a teen and their parents feel anxious and uneasy. Your child may be with someone you aren't familiar with. I had to rely on my teenagers to make wise decisions in these trying times, and let my teens know I valued their opinion and trusted them to decide responsibly. However, looking back at some of the decisions I made as a teen made me even more anxious.

My husband and I reacted to our children leaving home in unique ways. My husband encountered separation anxiety while I was happy our daughters were not away at college crying because of homesickness. It comforted my heart to know they moved into their new season with minimal effort.

Some parents may struggle to cope with the silence that fills the house when the children move away. Some experience empty-nest syndrome, a feeling of unhappiness and loneliness. Yet even when it feels hard to let go, the new and exciting experience of broadened horizons and the opportunity to practice making responsible adult choices are good for the grown child. This season is a reward for parenting and the doorway for the parent to transition into a place of rest from the intensity of raising children.

REFLECTION

The responsibilities in our lives are constantly growing and evolving. What does parenting look like when children still live in the home compared to when the house is empty? Does the role of a mother involve the same responsibilities as a grandmother? Each season requires individualized consideration. Coming up with a new identity can be as straightforward as picking a new name or as complex as attempting to rebuild your sense of self.

We are always growing and transforming. As we travel through life, God gives us the power to be whoever we need to be at every stage. Find and embrace the beauty in each season. When we savor the joy, we can look back with no regrets when the next period arrives.

PRAYER

Dear Lord,

I lift the next generation before you. Equip them as a powerful generation that will love you with their entire hearts, mind, soul, and body.

Like Queen Esther in Scripture, you have placed our children and grandchildren into this moment for such a time as this. Our world needs them, and they need your clarity, direction, and focus. Give them the boldness to stand for truth.

You have allowed us to be the elders in this season, and I pray my generation stands shoulder to shoulder with our children and grandchildren. Give us the grace to release our now adult offspring to the work you've called them to. Show us how to embody your encouragement and support for the younger generations. May our youth find confidence in knowing we believe in them and pray for them. Amen.

–CHAPTER 11–
SELF-CARE DURING TRANSITIONS

Not knowing how or when I would be triggered, I knew I needed to find solace in self-care, relaxation, and recovery. By taking care of myself, I was honoring Scott's memory in a meaningful way. One way for me to do this was to get a massage!

The sensation of the masseuse stretching and massaging my muscles was incredibly relieving, easing the tightness away. "Is there a particular area you want to focus on?" the massage therapist asked. My left shoulder was tense, and my neck ached, but I didn't want her to only hone in on those areas. My body craved the full experience.

I took a deep breath. The aroma of lavender essential oils soothed me. As I snuggled under the warm blanket, I felt its softness against my skin. The music in the room played at an optimal volume that was not too loud to be disturbing or too low to be inaudible. The therapist worked on my body, and her skilled hands kneaded out the knots in my muscles.

The silence in the spa room only amplified my thoughts as I lay on the massage bed, missing my husband. He was attentive to my likes and dislikes and tried to fulfill my wishes. Savoring the moment, I couldn't help but feel a tinge of sorrow mixed with sweetness. Every stroke from the masseuse's hands was a reminder of my husband's tender love and care for me. This massage had been made possible only months earlier on my fifty-ninth birthday when my husband organized a surprise party for me. My friends and family had left me with enough gift cards that I could keep coming back again and again.

Lying on the massage table, I could not help but wonder whether he was aware—when he was calling friends to come over and celebrate with me—that he only had a few months left with us. With each breath I took, sadness overwhelmed me. "Stay in the moment," I said to myself, breathing deeper, but my mind slipped back to the day of the party.

My fifty-ninth birthday had sneaked up on me. A few days before, we received the heartbreaking news my beloved brother had suddenly passed away. He was just two years older than I, and his wife asked me to give the eulogy. I was lost in thought until the sound of the doorbell ringing snapped me back to reality. The festivities began as people started parading in with their delicious food and thoughtful gifts. It was a beautiful gesture. Scott and I had previously agreed to wait until I turned sixty to have a joint party celebrating both of our birthdays. We'd come to this decision after being unable to celebrate our fiftieth birthday because Scott was one-month post-stem-cell transplant, and with a weakened immune system, hosting a party was not an option.

I guess he decided he couldn't wait because, on my fifty-ninth birthday, the sound of laughter echoed off the walls as my friends and family strolled through the door. No matter how many times I told him I didn't like surprises, he persisted in planning them because he enjoyed the thrill.

Everyone seemed to know about my favorite way of relaxing, and I suspected my husband was the one who blabbed. The day was amazing. Joy filled my heart—I couldn't have asked for a better celebration. It was truly a day to cherish.

In the days immediately following my husband's death, I tended to practical matters that needed my attention, to find solace in the sense of control and temporary distraction from grief: Letting family and friends know what was going on. Preparing for the funeral services was overwhelming, besides managing all the other tasks that come with someone's passing.

My sister invited me to go away with her a few weeks after Scott died, and I had mixed emotions about it, grappling with feelings of attachment and the fear of letting go. The push to move forward and the pull to hold on were two opposing forces I had to reconcile: Back—and—forth. Should I venture out and create fresh memories or remain in the comfort of familiar surroundings?

Without my husband, I felt like I was standing in the middle of a crowded room but completely alone and exposed. Absent his emotional support, I felt a sense of insecurity I hadn't experienced before. I reminded myself to take it slow and be kind to myself.

Opulence and extravagance surrounded us at the beautiful hotel where we stayed during our weekend getaway. The accommodations, which provided a comfortable and relaxing experience with their soft bedding and high-end amenities, impressed me. But the warmth of my sister's company made everything else pale in comparison.

The sense of calm and peace I felt upon returning home was proof the trip had been worthwhile. I gave myself permission to experience the full spectrum of emotions, allowing myself to feel both the lows of sadness and the highs of happiness.

When I didn't sleep well at night, I made sure to catch up on rest with a daytime nap. I remembered from my nursing training that sleep played a critical role in the healing process. The nights felt endless and ominous, but the warmth of the sun during the day brought some comfort.

Cooking has never been my forte, but I try to be intentional about eating nutritious meals. Well-balanced meals have a positive impact on a person's mood and energy level. Despite the difficult times, I made a conscious effort to nourish my body with the nutrients it needed. To keep my body healthy, my sister, a nutritionist, urged me to stay hydrated. Without proper hydration, fatigue, and lethargy can become more pronounced.

If I take a short walk from my front door, I can relax in the large gazebo and enjoy the peaceful view of the huge pond. This is not a place for swimming, but a sanctuary for those seeking solitude and inner peace. The serene setting of this place fosters a meditative atmosphere, perfect for reflecting on life's changes. Maybe it's because this is where our community prayer group meets twice a week that the atmosphere feels so comforting.

There's a beach nearby, just a few miles up the road from my house. Something about the water's gentle ebb and flow always puts me in a state of tranquility that feels almost divine. Whether it's a river, a lake, the ocean, or a pond, being near water seems to stimulate my creativity and bring clarity to my thoughts.

The warmth of the sun on my skin makes me feel alive as I walk outside. Whether it's listening to music, sermons, or talking to God, I find that it helps me release stress and uplifts my mood. I knew that during this transition, I might feel like withdrawing, but I needed to remind myself to stay connected. Reaching out to my supportive community comforted me. The weight of grief can make it difficult to find pleasure in even the simplest things. Spending time with my loved ones gave me a chance to catch my breath and feel like everything was going to be okay.

Grief can be sort of like a woman giving birth. The uterine contractions are robust and come quickly. There are short periods of rest in between contractions, and women become exhausted during this phase. The woman in labor has the promise of a baby when she makes it through the transitional phase. The pain is intense, and there may be moments when she thinks, "I can't do this."

In addition to the intense pain, some women experience waves of nausea and may vomit. Their bodies may tremble, and they might feel a sudden sensation of heat or cold. The long birth process can leave them feeling irritable and wondering when it will finally be over. The presence of loved ones and experienced medical staff can make a big difference for a woman in labor.

Despite the pain experienced with grief, along with other physical symptoms, there's a promise of a brighter day. My grief came in waves, and in the brief moments of rest, I clung to those memories of peace.

During my transitional seasons, I knew to prioritize my care. I needed the support of others. Coping with anxiety and uncertainty is a challenge many people face in life, so what are some helpful strategies one can use to manage these emotions? To navigate through this challenging situation, I relied heavily on the promises of the Bible and sought guidance from both my family and trusted professionals. The counselor's voice had a soothing quality, which gave me a sense of reassurance. A pastor or church leader, who has had specialized training in counseling, can provide valuable advice. Sharing their own experiences of loss, good friends and others who have gone through similar situations were a source of comfort for me. It's amazing how God can bring the right people into your life just when you need them most. Without the love and support of my family and friends, I may have gotten stuck in transition.

Managing my expectations became easier when I set achievable goals for myself. I made it a priority to avoid overcommitting myself and saying no to obligations that might add to my stress levels. Despite being in ministry, I felt the need to take some time away. Still feeling fragile, I stepped back from anything that would put me in front of a crowd. By putting my thoughts and feelings down on paper, I was able to gain a fresh perspective and make sense of my emotions.

My mother's favorite saying was that God won't give us more than we can handle. I couldn't help but think that God might be privy to information I wasn't. With his help, I could find a group of people who could help carry the load surrounding me with their kindness and strength. Loved ones reminded me I was not alone. Trekking through the initial days of anguish, however demanding, I had my community. Although I wanted to give back to the community that had given me so much, I realized this was the time for me to receive. Though I knew there would come a time when I would help others through tough seasons, for today, I sought solace in the familiarity of my village.

Do Something Different

I dedicated my time to caring for my husband and children for years, but now I needed a new routine to adapt to this season of life. I discovered the best way to honor the memory of my husband was by doing things that made me happy.

We couldn't help but feel a sense of loss during our first Christmas without Scott. He eagerly anticipated this holiday every year. It was the one he looked forward to the most. The moment November arrived, he'd start pulling out the decorations, sometimes sooner. His Christmas village was a wonderland of twinkling lights, miniature churches, hotels, and other buildings, including tiny people. As the holiday season approached, he transformed our home with decorations, sights, and smells of Christmas. The house was alive with the holiday spirit, with every nook and cranny adorned with wreaths, garlands, and other holiday trimmings. The presentation was key for Scott. When the neighbors stopped in, my husband, beaming from ear to ear, eagerly invited them to see his elaborate Christmas village.

Every year, we looked forward to spending Christmas at home, where we could enjoy the customary highlights and sounds of the holiday season. That was exactly how Scott wanted it. The year our first child was born, we made a trip to visit his family in New York. "There's nothing like being surrounded by my family," he said, "but next year, let's stay home." And so began our tradition.

To move forward, my grief counselor recommended we do something out of the ordinary this year. "Why not try starting a new routine?" he asked. "It helps with the grief."

So I made reservations for a cruise trip with my daughters. This was definitely different from what we were used to. It thrilled my sister and her family to join us aboard the cruise ship, taking part in all the fun activities. We were excited to take part in the ugly sweater competition, but the young adults didn't share our enthusiasm. We kept ourselves busy with a variety of activities, such as attending shows, exercising, and shopping.

I hung our Christmas stockings from the counter in my stateroom with great care, looking forward to the joy they would bring. The endless expanse of the ocean greeted my daughters and me as we opened our eyes on Christmas morning. As my daughter read the Christmas story, her voice echoed through the small cabin. The prayer of thanksgiving preceded the excitement of opening presents with a peaceful moment. Our family gathered, but one was missing.

It delighted us to make going on a Christmas trip every year a new routine. I realized I needed to cherish every moment because the girls would soon live their own lives. Maryland was the destination for our next adventure, which took place the following year. The Christmas feast was a lively affair with about thirty family members coming together. The sounds of laughter and chatter filled every corner of the house.

Excitement filled the room with the warmth of generosity and the sound of wrapping paper rustling. Family members came from far and near; it was wonderful. Quite different from our past Christmases.

When the following year arrived, a standstill had taken hold of everything: COVID-19.

We planned our virtual Christmas family celebration. "Let's wait for everyone to arrive before we start opening gifts," I suggested, hoping to avoid leaving anyone out. The feel of the soft Christmas pajamas and the warmth of the Santa hats brought a sense of joy to the Zoom room. We settled on this option since it was the most practical, considering we all lived hours away. We all agreed the risk of getting stranded somewhere was too high. It was a wise decision not to take any unnecessary health risks. It seems almost unreal to me now, reflecting on how we lived for such a long time.

The warmth of the smiles on their faces was visible on-screen as we finished the Christmas story and said prayers of gratitude before moving on to opening gifts. In my new season, we celebrated Christmas away from home in a different location, and virtually, but one thing remained constant. Before we opened our gifts, we took time to read the Christmas story and offer a prayer. That's how I grew up. That's how Scott did it, and that was a tradition worth holding on to—one none of us wanted to leave behind as we moved forward.

PHYSICAL CARE

Checking the time, I couldn't help but feel like I had been waiting in the exam room for hours. The minutes felt interminable, each second dragging on and on. It was not my favorite time of the year but a necessary time. Yearly exams with my primary and other doctors were due.

The knock was gentle, almost hesitant, but it still made

my heart race. Dr. Jacobs opened the door with precision and stepped into the room. Her kind personality is just as stunning as her physical features. I braced myself for her inevitable first question.

"How is your family?" she asked, her kind eyes looking up from the iPad. Over the years, she had become more than just a doctor to me. Living in the same community, we frequently crossed paths with her.

"After losing Scott, how have you been coping?" Tears welled up in my eyes. Recalling the trick my friend told me that would stop tears from falling. I lifted my head, trying to blink them away. Is there any chance they will stop? The mere mention of his name caused the fountain to spring to life, water cascading down my cheeks. "Are you sleeping well? If you require any medication, please let me know."

I had trusted her with my health concerns for a long time, as she had been my doctor for many years. Over the last decade of Scott's life, my caregiver's duties posed challenges in prioritizing my health. Despite this, my doctors were accommodating, offering flexible hours to ensure I didn't miss any appointments. I remained committed to not letting my health suffer, and Dr. Jacobs provided invaluable help in managing my physical care.

According to a published article, "The job of a caretaker can be stressful and isolating. Unfortunately, 30% of family caregivers die before the person they are caring for."[1] When I was a caregiver, at the first sign of trouble, I scheduled an appointment. I was determined to survive my caregiver years. If I didn't, it wouldn't be because I hadn't done my part.

Now that my caregiving days were over, I was more committed than ever to doing my part to stay healthy. After the exam, Dr. Jacobs hugged me and said, "I'll see you next year."

I had one more appointment. The prospect of being in

another doctor's office left me feeling overwhelmed, knowing she would certainly ask the same questions Dr. Jacobs asked, and I would break down in tears. The thought of having to answer the dreaded question with Dr. Roy, my primary physician, made me apprehensive, given my experience with Dr. Jacobs a few weeks earlier. Seeing her also for the first time as a widow was a powerful and overwhelming experience.

Dr. Roy's compassionate gaze as she entered the exam room affected me deeply even before she uttered a single word. "How are you holding up?" she inquired. I tried to dab away the tears, but they kept streaming down my face. "I'm going through a transition. Despite the present circumstances, I believe I will be okay." Dr. Roy sat with me, her presence offering a sense of calm and support as I tried to regain my composure.

"Considering the significant loss you've experienced, it is good to see you are taking care of yourself, and I have no doubt you will continue to do so," she said. I had no other choice but to do my best to stay healthy. My husband was gone, and that left me to navigate life on my own. My children were left with only me as their parent. While my mind was preoccupied with adjusting to the new season, I remained vigilant for any physical changes that may have been taking place in my body.

She gave me a thorough examination, analyzing every detail. In addition to checking my vitals, the doctor checked my ears, nose, and throat. As she placed the stethoscope on my chest to listen to my heartbeat, I noticed it had quickened. The toll of grief can cause physical discomforts, such as heart palpitations and shortness of breath. "Inhale deeply and exhale slowly," she instructed.

"Is there any pain?" she asked cautiously, pressing on various parts of my body. First, she checked the right side, then she checked the left. "Follow my fingers, smile, open your eyes, now close them." She touched my feet, feeling for swelling. "Straighten out your legs." A thump with the percussion hammer showed my reflexes were intact. She checked for a strong pulse in my extremities, not wanting to miss anything. "Your lab work is normal. The results of the mammogram showed no signs of abnormalities. A thorough assessment shows everything is in good shape." Yes. I was done with checkups until the next year.

It's common to feel overwhelmed during transition periods, but prioritizing self-care can make a significant difference. Continually giving of yourself while receiving nothing in return can have a detrimental effect on your mental and physical well-being. As a nurse, I have observed the undeniable relationship between emotional stress and physical sickness. The all-consuming nature of our experiences can cause us to neglect our own self-care and well-being, which is why it is important to take a step back and prioritize our health.

REFLECTIONS

What are some new traditions you would like to start? Have you neglected your health in any area: physical, emotional, or spiritual? What can you do to be more in tune with your body and take better care of yourself? Who is a part of your community? Think about an area you struggle with related to self-care, maybe it's eating properly or getting enough sleep, etc. Could you benefit from an accountability partner? What are some of your favorite things to do for yourself?

PRAYER

Dear Lord,

Thank you, Father. I am grateful to have been blessed with good health, a loving family, and faithful friends. I prioritize taking care of my physical well-being. The body is a sanctuary for the Holy Spirit. I am yours, not my own. Help me cultivate love and endurance for all you have trusted me with. I trust you to provide me with some insight on how to distinguish between situations where I need to take a step back and those where I should decline.

I deeply appreciate your concern for my well-being, and I know you want me to be in good health. I am committed to taking all the necessary measures to maintain my health. In my prayer, I ask for complete healing and protection from any sickness.

Your blessings have provided me with a network of family and friends who are always there to support me. My focus is on doing things that light up my heart and make me feel alive. Amen.

–CHAPTER 12–
ACCEPT A NEW SEASON

It had been months, and I still felt a deep uneasiness as I struggled with my lost state and lack of clarity about my future.

"Take it easy," my friends advised. "Be gentle and patient with yourself."

Yet, I wanted to push myself harder. By now, I reasoned, I ought to be feeling better. But beginning new projects proved frustrating. I had difficulty concentrating. Apathy weighed heavily, bringing its unwelcome companion, exhaustion. Each morning, anxiety and dread filled my stomach as I remembered I was alone. Scott was not coming back. Life was forever altered.

On my first Sunday back to church after my husband died, I wore a cheerful, bright-colored dress. What was I supposed to wear? What were the rules for this situation? Whenever someone commented on my clothing or appearance, I put on a brave face, but inside I trembled.

At last, I connected with my friend Edna, who was also a widow. In her religious community, women don specific-colored garments and shawls as a symbolic expression of mourning until the funeral proceedings conclude. These cultural norms helped people understand what is expected of them. Within these parameters, Edna and those in her situation could comfortably know what to do or at least know what to wear.

How long would this deep sadness linger? Would I be forever paralyzed, caught between two places? The lack of my husband's presence by my side and in my home was palpable. I strained to remember the gentle sound of his voice, my mind searching for the faintest hint of a memory.

I was immediately drawn to him when we met on the phone all those years ago. Scott's voice was warm and inviting. Hearing his name brought a lump to my throat. Was I being too rigid with myself by creating an ambitious timeline?

Uncertainty enveloped me. How should I proceed between this season of grief and a season of progress? The thought of burying my grief to move forward was a lie I had to unlearn. I thought I had to compartmentalize my sorrow neatly in a bundle before I could accept something else. However, perhaps it was possible to reach my goals while also honoring my grief.

Though lonely, I reminded myself I was making progress. Grief is a journey. When I realized this, a soft breeze of acceptance filled me. Amid grief, I came to terms with the incompleteness that lingered in my mind. After all, I had lost a significant part of who I had been for over one-quarter of a century, almost half of my life. I couldn't set my emotions aside and move onward. I would have to bring my feelings with me.

I would look back fondly on the happy memories we had made together as a family, but the sorrow of the moments we would never experience with him weighed heavily on my heart. When our daughters married, he wouldn't be there. Scott would have been honored to walk them down the aisle. I had to be at peace with the knowledge many cornerstone events would come that Scott would not be part of. His absence would continue to be keenly felt.

I was no longer a wife after twenty-seven years of marriage. The last decade of our lives together had been focused on caring for Scott. He was my husband, so what else would I do? Making a conscious decision, I devoted my life to making sure he was comfortable. Like a loop that constantly played in my thoughts was the question, "What am I supposed to do now?"

A Time to Mourn

"There is a time for mourning and there is a time to dance," says Ecclesiastes 3:4. This Scripture serves as a reminder that regardless of how difficult life is, there is always hope. Things will eventually change. Sorrow will end sooner or later.

Widowhood isn't something women seek, but death comes to all. An August 2017 article states there are 13.6 million widows in America, and about 700,000 women become widows in the US each year.[1] According to the US Census Bureau, the average age of widowhood is fifty-nine years old. According to statistics, I'm average.

My husband and I had planned to mark our sixtieth birthdays with a joyous celebration. Despite my reluctance, I celebrated my sixtieth birthday without him, knowing it was what Scott would have wanted. It was a difficult choice, but I ultimately decided that hosting the party was an essential part of my acceptance journey. Life continued to move forward, even amid the grief and loss I felt for someone I loved. As I took a deep breath, I felt a sense of determination fill me, and I knew I could carry on without my husband by my side.

As a widow, I was granted autonomy I had not been familiar with in a long time. I had devoted my time and energy to ensuring my husband was cared for. Suddenly, all the tasks that had been almost more than I could keep up with were gone. Instead of moving through the myriad responsibilities that went into tending to my husband and running our household, I looked around for something that needed to be done. In the stillness, I realized, *No one needs me.*

Didn't this also mean I was free to do whatever I wanted? There was no one to answer to. I had the liberty to leave home whenever I desired with no pressure of a set time of return. Although intriguing, the newly found freedom felt perplexing. I had been comfortable with structure. All my activities and decisions were based on what I thought my husband would need. I was alone now.

"It's time," my friend Ann said warmly, "to follow your heart."

What did that mean?

Taking care of Scott gave me a feeling of contentment. He was in heaven, so what was my role now? Who would I be in charge of tending to? I didn't know what step to take next.

My husband was a good man. Who I had become was so much about what he poured into me. He had sufficiently fulfilled his kingdom assignment as a godly husband, doing whatever he could to assist me in being everything that God had chosen me to be. And he'd done it seemingly effortlessly.

In Matthew's gospel, when Jesus was asked why his disciples did not fast, Jesus answered, "Can the wedding guests mourn as long as the bridegroom is with them? The day will come when the bridegroom is taken from them, and then they will fast" (9:15). Jesus spoke of being with his disciples, and while things were good and they were happy, there was no need for them to seek what they already had. As long as my husband affirmed and encouraged me, there was no lack. But when he died, I experienced want.

Could I blossom in my new season? After taking on the responsibility of being a caregiver, the time had come to put myself first. In this new season, God was using my situation to teach me how to trust him in a way I had never done before.

There was no escaping the heartbreak of the loss. The nights of watching the clock move from hour to hour became my norm. One night, I would sleep, and the next night, I wouldn't.

Scott was the strongest advocate of every endeavor I ever attempted. He was the one I bounced ideas off, even in my writing. He was quick to help with my research, make phone calls, arrange appointments, or do whatever his hands could find to do.

When I traveled or attended events, he wanted to know every detail when I returned. "How did it go? Who did you meet? How many people were there? How were the book sales? What did you speak about?"

Now no one waited at home to converse with me. There was no one to get excited about what I did, no one to assist me, no one to cheer me onward. I was not prepared to live life without my champion.

And I didn't want to.

No one could push me if I wasn't ready. Being a widow was a distinction I never chose, and I had a decision to make. I could seek joy in what I faced or remain stuck with feelings of pity and sorrow.

TRANSITION

Those in this season require time to heal. The amount of time needed depends on the individual. When a woman is in labor and reaches the transition phase, the time varies from mother to mother. This phase of labor is the most forceful and strenuous phase for most women, and also the shortest.

Many things can keep us stuck and not wanting to move forward. Sometimes, we wait for others to permit us to forge ahead. I realized I didn't have to wait for anyone's permission. I could move past those feelings of inadequacy and lack. Without my husband to encourage me and tell me that it was okay to enter this next season, I could tell myself, "I can do this, I have to."

Knowing in my heart God promised not to leave me alone did not replace the loneliness and vulnerability I felt. But it would one day soon.

It would have been easy for me to get caught in one place because I was unwilling to experience rejection, hurt, disappointment, or other unfavorable emotions. But when I try to bury those feelings instead, I know that I must face them and work through the pain to get to my next point in the journey.

To comprehend acceptance, I used my mental capacity to recognize the difficulties of grief. I grasped the idea that life is fleeting. Seasons change, and moving with the flow makes change more tolerable.

EVOLUTIONS

The intricacies of change can sometimes lead to confusion and unexpected outcomes, which can have devastating consequences. But they can also be liberating. How I respond to alterations can relate to how I see myself. The words I speak demonstrate who I am. The way I think about change influences how I go about tackling new experiences. It's my choice; I have the ability to train myself to react in a certain way.

When something occurs out of the ordinary, my norm is to react in a programmed, almost mechanical way. There was a tendency for me to impose standards on myself that did not align with the Bible's teachings. Some of my Christian friends told me, "People are watching you; be strong."

The Bible speaks of death and the emotions that come with it. The Old Testament recounts how Jacob was inconsolable over the loss of his son, Joseph. In Genesis 37, Joseph's brothers sell him into slavery and deceive their father Jacob by presenting Joseph's blood-stained coat as evidence of his death. The loss of a child, especially through such a tragic and violent incident, would likely have been a source of immense sorrow for any parent. I imagine Jacob had questions, "Did my son suffer?" "Did he die instantly?" Jacob was devastated.

David's deep grief over the anticipated loss of his baby son is indeed an example of grief in Scripture (2 Samuel 12). He fasted, prayed, and refused to leave his house, hoping that God would spare his child's life. However, despite David's fervent prayers, the child became ill and eventually died.

David grieved when Saul and Jonathan were killed. David and Jonathan's friendship is indeed a significant story in the book of Samuel. Jonathan was the son of King Saul, and despite the differences in their backgrounds and circumstances, he and David developed a deep, genuine friendship. Their bond was so strong it transcended societal expectations and challenges.

When Saul and Jonathan were killed in battle, David mourned their deaths deeply. His grief was particularly profound for Jonathan, his dear friend. The grief and honor David felt for Jonathan are demonstrated in various ways, including David's lamentation in 2 Samuel 1. In addition to expressing his sorrow, King David sought to honor Jonathan's memory. He inquired as to how he could show kindness to the house of Saul for Jonathan's sake. Jonathan's lame son Mephibosheth became the recipient of David's generosity because of the love David had for his father (2 Samuel 9).

The prophet Isaiah introduces us to the Messiah's grief: "He was despised and rejected by men, a man of sorrows and acquainted with grief, and as one from whom men hide their faces he was despised, and we esteemed him not" (Isaiah 53:3). Jesus knew the pain of rejection by those he came to save.

Showing emotions when grieving does not demonstrate a lack of faith. In John 11:35, Jesus wept at Lazarus's tomb. "Jesus is fully God, but he is also fully human. Two natures in one person, unmixed forever. Even though he knew he was about to perform the miracle, he grieved with the pain and sorrow as well as the death-dealing effects of sin on those he loves."[2]

Hebrews 4:15 tells us, "For we do not have a high priest who is unable to sympathize with our weaknesses, but one who in every respect has been tempted as we are, yet without sin." Jesus endured suffering and hardships. Because he knows how we feel, he can help us.

I didn't want to rush grief; it takes as long as it takes. Grief is a necessary emotion that comes with the loss of a loved one, and those who feel the pain of grief should be able to express the feeling openly. Having support from those who respect and celebrate each individual's distinct journey is important. After my experience of grief, I am more aware of the needs of others who are mourning, giving them the time and space to process their sorrow. The challenge is to not let grief become consuming. A grief counselor provided a listening ear, helping me express my feelings and accept strategies for moving on.

Grief is expressed in many ways from tears to silence. What caused the death? How old was the deceased, and how many years had the relationship lasted? Did the death come as a shock or was the loss expected? When a loved one dies, the pain of loss can be difficult to process. The grief of a sudden, traumatic death can be paralyzing, and even the grief of death from natural causes can be overwhelming.

The heartache and hardship a person experiences from other losses can impact a present loss. For some, they have already experienced the aching void of losing a family member. For others, this is their initial encounter with grief. Every memory, feeling, and experience someone has had up to the point of losing a loved one can shape the way they respond to current loss.

Scripture teaches in 1 Thessalonians 4:13, "But we do not want you to be uninformed, brothers, about those who are asleep, that you may not grieve as others do who have no hope." Paul brings clarity that when believers die, they will rise to eternal life. Apparently, the people Paul speaks to in this Scripture were confused about death in Christ and believed that dead Christians would miss the Lord's coming. Paul's explanation sheds light on how believers express grief. He is not saying Christians should not grieve, but that we can grieve with hope because of the pending glorious second coming of the Lord. As Christians, we can freely express our grief, yet we have hope in Christ Jesus that one day we will be reunited with our loved ones. When I start to feel lonely, I remind myself of this hope.

"Paul knows how dangerous ignorance can be; therefore, he doesn't want the Thessalonians to be uninformed. An ignorant Christian can become a hopeless Christian. To know the truth is to be set free from the hopelessness of ignorance."[2]

I'm unable to describe the different ways people express their grief over a loss. Every woman confronts widowhood uniquely. She steps in with an understanding that's only familiar to her, a feeling no one else may be able to comprehend. The memories of her childhood and the way she was brought up may influence her grieving process. Maybe her husband was the first man she felt a strong connection with. Maybe she never had a strong bond of commitment from a father.

Sometimes grief may be impacted by growing up without a father to speak into her life and help her discover her identity in her formative years. Others may grow up with a hesitancy towards men, a guardedness she couldn't shake. Still, others grieve for the life partner who provided support and advice, and the husband who helped mold her as a wife and mother.

The widow's age plays an important role in the grief process. If she is young, her grief may be profound for all she will never experience. Maybe she hasn't witnessed the miracle of birth yet. The younger widow may have a remarriage in the future. Though a second spouse will not take the place of first love, amid sorrow, a new soulmate brings fresh joy and companionship.

A widow's grief may be impacted by the ages of her children, whether they are young or grown up. Did the marriage have a firm foundation of trust and respect, or was the marriage full of mistrust and hurt? Will the family struggle to make ends meet without the money that the spouse brought in? Was the husband the sole provider of financial support for the family?

External factors can complicate grief. If there are young children in the home, the widow has a continual responsibility for them. Finding her way through the darkness and confusion of the children's grief is nuanced while she is still dealing with her own. If children are grown up with families of their own, the widow, her children, and the families of her children may experience loneliness. Feeling solitary, it is commonly a struggle to come to terms with the new identity as a widow.

MOVE ON

Though grief may be a shared experience, each person feels their grief differently and adopts ways to cope. For some wives, the idea of taking on a leadership role in managing those areas her husband typically oversaw is unfamiliar and unnerving. Different cultures have distinct traditions for paying their respects. I believe the widow's attitude and outlook will be a deciding factor in the way she handles her sorrow. Faith can provide comfort and guidance in times of grief.

When a crisis strikes, it's important to be mindful of our mental health. My healing process required that I give myself space to understand what was happening. How does an individual stay true to themselves amidst the ever-changing nature of life? People can spend years searching for meaning and direction in their lives. Every person is driven by the need to uncover who they truly are.

As we move through our formative years, our careers and big decisions contribute to how we settle our identity. What influence do transitions in life have to alter a person's identity?

Any adjustment can bring a feeling of uncertainty. Questions swirl, forcing us to reevaluate our current status. Significant changes challenge us to think critically and reconsider our current lifestyle. Changes often evoke powerful reactions of resistance. With all the changes I was facing, my core beliefs remained intact.

How would I know when I was ready to push aside the sorrow and get back on my feet?

Moving on in life doesn't mean the feelings fade away. The influence of the one I loved will always be a part of my daily life. In my grief journey, I refused to let anyone else dictate the way I should react.

"Take your time to process your emotions," I told myself.

In her book, *"Moving Forward on Your Own: A Financial Guidebook for Widows,"* Dr. Kathleen Rehl writes that "it wasn't supposed to turn out this way. When you married, you both promised it would last forever but it didn't. And now you are part of a growing demographic. Like your many other widowed sisters, years ago you didn't think much about the fact that you would probably outlive your husband, but most wives do."[3]

In my tight-knit circle of friends, there are five of the seven of us who have felt the profound emptiness that comes with the death of a husband. When we met nearly twenty years ago, only one of us was a widow. After enduring a lengthy illness, my husband passed away. For some of my friends, their loss was sudden and unexpected. Despite the age differences or the longevity of the illness, grief is grief. The pain is real and dictates a response.

Widows find themselves facing sudden responsibilities, which may lead to feeling overwhelmed and uncertain. I understand the deep sense of uncertainty and vulnerability that a widow may feel as she undertakes her first financial transaction. Familiarity is gone and she is now obligated to become acclimated to the new season. By embracing new opportunities, I gained valuable knowledge and insight into the world around me and into myself.

REFLECTION

What experience have you encountered in your life that can't be undone? What has helped you accept where you are now? Revisiting core values can help you redefine who you are in this new season. How have you come to terms with your new season and how different is it? God's plan for our lives doesn't change; it may look different in each season, but the overall purpose is connected to who he created you to be. Rest, knowing he's got you in his hands and no one can snatch you out.

PRAYER

Dear Lord,

I pray for those who find themselves in a place where the only thing to do is accept where they are. I ask you to grant them your peace to accept what they cannot change. Reassure them today that you are with them always. Just as you have been with me, I trust you will be with the reader of this prayer.

Your gentle whisper calmed my heart when I felt overwhelmed. Whisper grace, strength, and guidance for them in ways they'll recognize you. Send support and the love of families and friends. Affirm that you care, and you still have a plan and purpose for their lives. Help them not to become weary but give them strength to keep moving forward. Amen.

–CHAPTER 13–
CLARITY IN TRANSITION

In the hopes of gaining some valuable insights into what the future holds, I made my way back to the place Scott and I had called our home for more than two decades. The opportunity to revisit the area where we spent many happy years provided healing for me. I reconnected with family and friends, experiencing the warmth of their embrace. Being in a place with a flood of memories filled with laughter and joy gave me peace.

During the time we resided in Maryland, there were no health concerns regarding Scott's well-being. Those who knew us back then didn't know us in our roles as a patient and a caregiver. People saw us as a husband and wife raising two girls. To them, in that season of our lives, we were known and remembered as pastors in the neighborhood.

During my visit back home, I almost felt normal. I saw the effort and dedication each of these precious family and friends put forth in moving forward in their lives. Some were growing a ministry, some were nearing the end of their careers, others were starting over after the death of a spouse, and many were taking joy in their grandchildren. Despite pressure and pain, I watched people rejoice as they celebrated their birthdays and walked through doors of opportunity.

As I looked around, memories of Scott and I enjoying our early years together came flooding back, and I couldn't help but wonder, *what does the future hold for me?* What would this transition teach me? Could I use this lesson to help others? How could I use God's power to give comfort and hope to others and those around them? I was filled with anticipation as I readied myself to uncover what I sought. But I was still a widow.

Strong and Courageous

Does the pain of grief ever truly disappear? I don't have the answer to that yet, but I am finding solace in the journey. Grief doesn't follow a linear path, and there's no universally right way or time limit. I attempted to stay in the moment and process the sadness of my loss, the tears streaming down my face. Not trying to push the pain away. I knew from the start I would need to understand and feel various emotions to support others. As I slowly work through my grief, I'm creating a narrative to provide hope and solace to others, and through the process, I'm finding healing.

As I allowed myself to embrace change, my mind became liberated, and I began to experience life more fully. Looking back on when Scott selected me to be his wife brings me immense happiness, although that period is now in the past. I have fulfilled my commitments as his wife. I will always look back on our time together with immense love and fondness. But I will not give up, nor will I give up hope. We can always rely on the truth that God's blessings are limitless. The air surrounding me is alive with possibility because God is eternal, and I know he loves. Even when the world is in flux, God's steadfast plan for our lives remains constant.

As I pray to God, I can look forward to the guidance he provides for the future. Regardless of what season we are in, God's Word provides truth and rest.

Deuteronomy 31:6 says, "Be strong and courageous. Do not fear or be in dread of them, for it is the Lord your God who goes with you. He will not leave you or forsake you." The children of Israel were about to experience a transition. Moses was about to die, and Joshua would be the new leader. Moses encouraged the people, and the same encouragement applies to those of us in transition today. God will be with you. He will never leave you.

I found letting go brought a sense of liberation that benefits me and those in my circle. Appreciating the opportunities presented allowed me to continue forward. New possibilities opened up with the newfound choices.

Life transitions, like the loss of a loved one, a divorce, career loss, or becoming empty nesters, can provide opportunities to explore new activities. Launching children into adulthood is a huge transition for both the child and the parents. This change brings with it new opportunities for both parties that weren't available before.

Despite feelings of disorientation, every season is filled with beauty. I learned to take in all they offer. My life is more beautiful when I support and aid those in need. Even in the most challenging of times, coming alongside others is life-giving. The process of transitioning can lead to exciting new opportunities for businesses and ministries as God works all things for good.

Apostle Paul writes in Romans 8:28, "And we know that for those who love God all things work together for good, for those who are called according to his purpose." Our love for God teaches us to stay tuned in to him during hard times. The desperation we feel in moments of stretching forces us to draw closer to him. The purpose of God's will controls everything, and he works every detail of our lives for our good.

Sometimes we try to figure out how things will work, but the truth is we don't know how God will work all things together for good to those who love Him and are the called according to His purpose, but we must believe it. This precious promise is for those who love Him, and who have been called to serve

His purposes. The promise was made only to believers. But, for them, there could be no more reassuring one. How could *this* possibly work together for good? The verse doesn't say some things work together or even most things do, but, rather, *all things work together for good.*[1]

Life comes with lots of surprises, whether we are prepared or not. Cherishing the individuality God gives allowed me to see clearer the path he had for me. I acknowledged the pains of growth, so the pain wouldn't linger and become harder to cope with. Talking with a supportive friend and working with a counselor showed me how to embrace the changes life brings. Having someone to talk to who could offer advice and empathy impacted my day-to-day relationships as well as my future connections.

We can prepare financially and spiritually for loved ones leaving us. According to the Scriptures, it's clear that it is appointed unto man once to die and after that eternity, but can we really prepare emotionally? While Scott and I made plans for our eternal souls and financial plans for our family, emotionally neither of us wanted to let go.

I'm never ready for a good season to end. The tough seasons I want to be over fast. But in reality, I can never experience the comfortable season if I don't endure the uncomfortable ones.

SNOW IN SPRING

We lived up North for many years before moving to the South. The winters were often harsh, and we couldn't wait for spring to come. One year, it snowed on my birthday, March 24, as the cold weather lasted even after the season had changed. Technically my birthday is in the spring, but the snow said otherwise. How do I enter a new season but hold a residue from the previous season? While we carry something from every season of our lives, ironically the excess that lingers longest typically is the result of a bad season.

When I am in the transitions of life, even difficult ones, I try to remember one truth. This is temporary. Being widowed at fifty-nine was never something I would have chosen. Life changed in a split second. The transition may have caught me off guard, but nothing surprises God.

I didn't know where I would go from that point, but God did. I asked God to help me spotlight what was left, not what I lost. His plan was waiting for me to take hold of him.

Transition poses a problem when it breaks up what holds something together that is vital to our lives. When our foundation is secure, we are better able to move through the challenges of life without an identity crisis.

Some widows choose to stay in their family homes. Others start fresh. After three years, I sold the home we shared as a family for nearly eighteen years. I thought selling the house would be hard, leaving all the memories, but it wasn't. I was ready.

My struggle came as I prepared to buy another home. Fear of making an unwise choice plagued me. I couldn't allow fear to keep me from deciding. I'd come too far and was determined not to go backward. After praying, I trusted that God was with me and could continue to be with me wherever I decided to live.

Widows sometimes have difficulty worshiping at the same church they attended when their husbands sat at their side. Although it took a bit of effort, I eventually found my way back to the sanctuary, feeling grateful for its comforting presence. A desire to be close to the people who had known and loved my husband deeply motivated my decision to stay at my current church. Sitting on the opposite side of the church gave me a fresh viewpoint. It was a seat my husband and I had never shared before. That minor alteration may have seemed insignificant, but it held great substance for me and my future.

God's plan for me may seem to be a mystery, but I have confidence he will reveal it when the time is right. Identity is not determined by geography. To navigate through times of transition successfully, being secure with who I am is of utmost importance. My belief is that with the trust I have in God, I can achieve success and flourish in all aspects of my life.

My approach to each day is expecting the unexpected. Just as summer changes to fall, life will change, sometimes without warning. How do we avoid planting our identity in a certain season? Is it possible not to settle in and become complacent? The larger issue is what can I glean in and from this classroom called life. Even when we don't want to be taught, there are valuable nuggets we pick up along the way. Whatever God allows into our lives, he has a plan. No challenge is absent from teachable moments.

It's easy to get relaxed, staying within the boundaries of our comfort zone, not wanting to go beyond it. Sometimes there is an illusion that staying in the boat assures our safety; however, our protection is contingent upon the condition of the boat we are on. Should the boat become faulty or malfunction, it is essential to disembark. I'm learning not to be rigid but letting myself be inspired to try something different. The greater the obstacle I face, the more opportunity I have to learn. Navigating all the adjustments that had to be made was difficult.

We may experience doubt when the unexpected occurs. A person may live their dream, married to the love of their life, with the ideal career, but then the company goes out of business. Unemployment can change the dynamics of every relationship. Illness within the family shifts priorities. These transitional moments cause us to either move forward or get stuck. The season will change, but it is up to us to evolve.

God's plan for us is always greater than the one we have for ourselves. When my life didn't turn out the way I wanted it to, I could still see the hand of God ordering my steps. The core of who he created us to be is still present, even when we have to search for it. God uses every experience to teach us something. He has a reason for everything he allows. God does not change his mind concerning the plans he has for his people when life changes course.

Seasons come and go but always come back around. There are valuable lessons to be learned along the way. You can revisit things that seem far out of your reach. There is a beauty yet left inside waiting to bud. It was important for me to learn how to nourish what God placed in me. I learned to rest in him by spending time in his Word.

What I was to become wasn't immediately clear to me. As I grew, I could see that everything I considered a failure was an opportunity to assume a new viewpoint. There will be failures and missed opportunities along the way, but even in that, maturity is taking place. It's never easy to lose someone you love, but having something to think about can make it more bearable. Some widows have a job to go back to, and that brings with it a feeling of accomplishment, unlike the wife whose husband was the center of her life. When we plant our identity in a temporary season of life, it often causes challenges to arise when that season has passed.

Losing a job creates a sudden lifestyle change. Without warning, a layoff upends the comfortable stability of your job, leaving you reeling. How does one accept their current financial struggles and move forward? Just when friends became empty nesters, ready to enjoy free and private time, an aging parent came to live with them. The room just decorated as a sewing room had to be converted back to a bedroom for Mom or Dad.

Some seasons and transitions are good and welcome while others are difficult. Paul writes in Philippians 4:11–13:

Not that I am speaking of being in need, for I have learned in whatever situation I am to be content. I know how to be brought low, and I know how to abound. In any and every circumstance, I have learned the secret of facing plenty and hunger, abundance and need. I can do all things through him who strengthens me.

Paul was content in his current state. Though he may not have had more than others, his attitude stands out. Whatever Paul dealt with, he learned to be content and at peace with himself. Paul's trust was anchored in God, his mercy, and grace. Often difficult, but daily, I embrace this attitude to not let stress and fear take control.

Apostle Paul's unwavering faith was clear, even despite all the extreme circumstances he encountered. When we read his letters in Scripture, we can almost feel the anguish of his struggles. But he found his strength in his trust in Christ. He didn't take credit for his new attitude or his provisions. Paul was content and at ease, knowing he was in Christ, no matter the situation. I believe his contentment was in part due to his life experiences. He saw many struggles, but he learned to trust God in them all.

J. Vernon McGee writes:

Whatever Christ has for you to do He will supply the power. Whatever gift He gives you, He will give you the power to exercise that gift. A gift is a manifestation of the Spirit of God in the life of the believer. As long as you function in Christ, you will have power. He certainly does not mean that he is putting into your hands unlimited power to do anything you want to do. Rather, He will give you the enablement to do all things in the context of His will for you. (McGee, *Thru the Bible*, V:327–8).[2]

After facing any challenge, the invaluable lessons learned are the greatest reward. It is easy to feel like the surrounding walls are closing in as if the place you are today will always be your reality. Be assured that no season of life lasts forever. Learning to see the good in life helps us deal with the bad and moves us forward.

During the process of gathering information for this book, I heard many stories of people's experiences. Despite their differences, the individuals shared a common thread of connectedness. Being in their comfort zone gave them a sense of safety, but they understood that growth required them to step outside of it.

Every life switch is like unlocking a door, giving a sense of independence and possibility. When we assess the benefit of the outcome against the cost of what is being sacrificed, decisions can be made. Some conversions are predictable, such as when a child goes away to college. As parents convert into the empty nester season of life, the feeling of self-determination fills the air. When my children left for college, I missed them, feeling a deep sense of sadness at their departure, but there was also an exhilarating feeling of relief. As this fresh period begins, postponed dreams can be reexamined.

After years of attention to the children, parents can focus on themselves—things that they have always wanted to do. For some it may be to travel, for others, it may be to write a book. The good thing is, whatever it is, you now have the time to accomplish it. No more after-school activities that require you to be present, consuming your evening. Not that parents don't enjoy these moments, but after eighteen years, many have seen it all. From dance to sports. First day of school, first sleepover, first dates, and the list goes on and on. These are now memories, and parents can concentrate on enjoying their newfound freedom.

I remember my youngest daughter's last day of school. She attended an international baccalaureate program at a high school outside our neighborhood, about a thirty-minute drive when the traffic was good. On that final day, I don't know who was happier, me or her. It took me a while before I wanted to drive in that direction again. Carpooling was no longer my focus. That season had passed.

My friend Clara's sleeping patterns shifted once her youngest child left for college, allowing her to stay in bed longer. The absence of the early morning rush to meet the bus brought a sense of calm to their household. As she sipped her coffee, she felt a renewed sense of purpose for the new season. Being there for her children had always been important to her, and now she was thrilled to see them soaring.

For those of us living in temperate climates, a change in season can come without warning. Living in Maryland, I had grown accustomed to the gradual decrease in temperature during the month of September. As we observed the leaves change from green to brilliant yellow, orange, and red, the signs reminded us that a new season was quickly approaching. Although the leaves in Florida do not change color, the seasons still come and go throughout the year.

We often sit and wait for the visible signs of a changing season before we accept it. There may be no physical evidence yet that we can see, but we sense a new season is upon us. I was waiting for my grief to subside before I could move on, but eventually, I had to accept my loss and bring the pain with me into the next chapter of my life. I didn't know when the pain would end, but I knew God would give me the strength that I needed to move forward.

Finding joy in the process was intentional for me. For many days, I asked myself the question, "What can I do today that will bring me joy?" It's the simple things in life that can offer the most joy. Learning to move from one stage to the other gracefully is a good thing. I was married to Scott until death parted us. I want to always feel connected to him.

My heart hurts for couples who have been married for many decades and what the survivor goes through. The pain must be tremendous. Moving on takes courage and determination.

REFLECTION

Wherever you are in your process, take a moment to appreciate how far you have come. It's the small steps that turn into big ones. What can you do today that you weren't able to do yesterday? How did you sleep last night? Was it better than the night before? God is with you every step of the way. As you spend time with him, he will give you clarity regarding your next steps. He may send others to encourage you as you move forward. He may cause you to pay special attention to a beautiful flower, reminding you that life is still filled with beauty.

PRAYER

Dear Lord,

There are so many things I face in life, some things that take my breath away. But even in those moments, I recognize you are with me, and you promise you will never leave me. For those who have arrived at a state of acceptance, help them grasp that in this life there is pain, but your Word declares that you can rescue us from every one of our afflictions. "Many are the afflictions of the righteous, but the Lord delivers him out of them all" (Ps. 34:19). The Message translation reads, "Disciples so often get into trouble; still, God is there every time."

Grant me the power to stand. Thank you for those you have put around me to encourage me as I move forward.

Thank you, Lord, that no matter the obstacles and hardships, you can turn even the most arduous experiences into something meaningful. Even if everything is positive, there are still adjustments that need to be made. I believe there is a special place in your heart for widows. Show me the way to seek your guidance on the next steps I should take.

"God, grant me the serenity to accept the things I cannot change, courage to change the things I can, and wisdom to know the difference."[3] Accepting the inevitability of what happens is not easy. But I'm thankful for the grace, help, and power that you can give. Amen.

–CONCLUSION–

The best thing about seasons is they continue to change. Genesis 8:22 says, "While the earth remains, seedtime and harvest, cold and heat, summer and winter, day and night, shall not cease."

The promise we have from God is this, just as the seasons of the year never cease, so do the seasons of our lives. Even in the difficult season, we can look forward to the sunshine of spring. Psalm 30:5 says, "Weeping may tarry for the night, but joy comes with the morning." In times of misery and despair, life seems catastrophic, but the deliverance God provides far exceeds what we have endured.

Sometimes transitions make no sense at all. We cannot understand why God allows certain things. With our finite minds, we will never understand an infinite God, but let's try to put into perspective why some things happen.

How do we ensure we make excellent decisions while in the switching mode? Because of the stress that accompanies changeovers, it's easy not to think things through carefully. Unwise decisions cause regret later. Major shifts like divorce can cause a person to question their value and principles. I've never been divorced, but I've heard it's a death of a sort. We need strong people around us in those moments. Wise counsel can help bring hurting people from places of despair.

Without the proper support, people can get stuck and not move forward.

Just as our world is forever changing, so are we. As we grow both emotionally and in age, we learn from challenges and the experiences of others. Some of the moments of life I questioned as a young woman, pose no questions for me now as an older woman. I have simply lived long enough to witness the hand of God in many areas of my life, and my trust in him has grown. Life keeps moving forward, and I'm filled with expectancy of the unknown.

I am concerned about my future, but that doesn't mean I'm not looking forward to what's ahead. The delicate part is trying to comprehend all that lies ahead. Change is a reminder the hand of God is omnipresent, and the great realization God's Word is true gives me peace.

Even when life doesn't make sense, we can view things through the eyes of faith, reminding us that we can trust God. Regardless of the phase of life we are in or the journey we may be on presently, we can trust he has not left us to complete it alone.

Hebrews 13:5 says, "Keep your life free from the love of money, and be content with what you have, for he has said, I will never leave you nor forsake you." Knowing that the Lord is always with us gives us the solidity to enjoy everything he gives us. It also reminds us that his presence is better than any material possession.

God assures us through his Word. We know he cannot lie according to Numbers 23:19: "God is not man, that he should lie, or a son of man, that he should change his mind. Has he spoken, and will not fulfill it?" When God speaks, he doesn't have to use the word *promise* as we do. We know his Word is sure and cannot change. He will walk with us through every change we face in life.

In my dark moment, I didn't need to fear, for the strong, reassuring hands of a caring God crafted me. I tried to write this book four years ago, but it wasn't the season for me. Now that I'm in a new place emotionally, the time is now. God designed me to be resilient. He didn't just want me to survive, but to thrive in the face of life's trials.

When opposition comes, we seek to discover the message we are to receive. The goal is to emerge from the crisis as a more aware and determined human being. If we learn nothing, we must ask the question "Why?" Even in the face of an existential crisis, seek the good. If we believe that all things work together for our good then there must be something good coming.

In moments of questions and purpose, we may not always have the answer, but Scripture teaches in James 1:3: "For you know that the testing of your faith produces steadfastness." The word *steadfastness* speaks of endurance, perseverance, and being able to stand even in the greatest trials and sufferings. Testing strains us, cultivating our endurance. Seeing the enemy's attempts to tear us down only strengthened our resolve, leading to victory after victory.

I didn't know the level of my inner strength until I was challenged by the tumultuous storms of life. The storms remind me that when I embark on the journey to better myself, I must endure the discomfort that comes with growth. Many people want to advance in their careers without putting in the effort. Striving for a goal is a fundamental part of personal development.

If one arrives at the finish line and has not gone through the process, is there a true benefit? In the age of participation trophies, where everyone receives a prize for simply showing up, it can be easy to forget just how much effort is needed to accomplish a goal. If a racer simply shows up at the finish line without running the race, would that person deserve the medal? No. If there is no effort then the process of winning means nothing. There is no personal fulfillment in receiving a prize for something you didn't accomplish.

When someone takes a shortcut, there is no knowledge or skill to pass on that would help another. I had to confront the pain of my husband's absence. I could have tried to distract myself with work and hobbies, never having to confront the anguish of my grief. But when a widow approached me, her eyes full of silent desperation, what could I offer in response? I had to embrace the ache of my heartache and recognize the impact of the loss on my new beginning, preparing me to minister to others.

Scott taught me that every person adds something to your life. He showed me how to look beyond what a person looks like and what they say and really see them for who they are.

I am more aware of the importance of the people God puts in my life and the wisdom they can impart.

When I take the time to communicate with people, I've noticed I gain a fresh outlook on my issues, which helps me find solutions and progress. After listening to others, the image I see differs vastly from what I had originally assumed. Connecting with one another helps us gain perspective as we navigate new seasons.

Was I willing to walk through the hurt and pain of loss to enter my new season? Sometimes we get trapped because we are unwilling to experience the atmosphere of rejection, hurt, and disappointment to get to our next season.

I had to grapple with the fact the lonely season of widowhood was all mine to accept or reject. I could tell myself all day long I was still married to Scott, but the reality is I wasn't anymore. Although I still feel married to him, I'm not sure how long I will feel this way. But for now, I embrace where I am and depend on God to carry me through. Moving through pain takes time and some need more time than others.

My pastor shared insights I hadn't considered. My friends and other women who had lost spouses shared their support. They helped me get through the toughest phase.

Coming home after a long trip is still hard for me. I wanted my husband to be here with me, but I had to accept he was at peace, and I had to be too. Living each day to the fullest is my goal. That's what Scott would want for me, and it is definitely what I want for myself.

This is my reality, and I welcome it with wonder and expectation. I'm moving forward while carrying the memories of my past. Each day, my life feels more balanced and fulfilled. While it's natural to feel a mix of emotions when facing the unknown, God is with me. I'm excited about future possibilities and new experiences. Every step I take forward is a chance to create new memories and build upon the foundation of my past.

No longer am I afraid to say the words aloud: "Yes, I am a widow."

Dear Reader,

I lay my heart bare in the pages of this book. May the things I shared encourage you. I started praying for you five years ago and continue to pray for you. God has great things for you in your new season. Don't be afraid to take a step. I know what it's like to be anxious about the future. We don't know what is ahead, but God does.

I believe my latter days will be greater than my former, and I pray the same for you. As we move from one season to the next, we will experience frustrations. Should we lower our expectations to avoid disappointment? No. But we can learn to manage our expectations. Our best guesses about what the future holds may be off the mark. The eventual result usually is a surprise to us. God's ways are vastly higher than our own.

Let's go find out what our next season holds. With God, we can do anything. Change can be unique and beautiful. Ask God to open your eyes to what you can offer to someone else.

We are God's creations, made in his image. You are valuable to him. The experience of this current season is necessary for where God wants to take you. Stand strong, your story is still being written.

Dr. Evelyn Johnson-Taylor

NOTES

Introduction

1. Jewish Publication Society, *Tanakh: The Holy Scriptures* (Philadelphia: Jewish Publication Society, 1985), Eccl. 3:1.

2. *Merriam-Webster*, s.v. "transition (*n*)," accessed 1 December 2013, https://www.merriam-webster.com/dictionary/transition.

Chapter 2—Personality Impacts Transitions

1. Tim LaHaye, *Transforming Your Temperament*. (New York: Inspirational Press, 1991), 12.

2. Linda Gilden and Linda Goldfarb, *Linked Maximizing Life Connections One Link at a Time*. (Friendswood, Texas: Bold Vision Books, 2018), 75.

3. Gary R. Collins, Ph.D., *Christian Counseling: A Comprehensive Guide* (Nashville, TN: Thomas Nelson, 2007), 760–761.

Chapter 4—Two Become One

Denise and Barbara Rainey, *Building Your Mate's Self-Esteem*. (Nashville, TN: Thomas Nelson Publishers, 1995), 192–193.

Chapter 5—Prepare For Transition

1. John D. Barry et al., *Faithlife Study Bible* (Bellingham, WA: Lexham Press, 2012, 2016), Dt. 6:8–9.

2. Dr. Henry Cloud and Dr. John Townsend, *Boundaries*

When to Say Yes When to Say No To Take Control of Your Life. (Grand Rapids, MI: Zondervan, 1992), 79.

3. "Learning New Skills Keeps an Aging Mind Sharp," *Association for Psychological Science—APS*, 21 Oct. 2013, www.psychologicalscience.org/news/releases/learning-new-skills-keeps-an-aging-mind-sharp.html.

Chapter 6—Regret in Transition

1. Gary Chapman, *The 5 Love Languages: The Secret to Love That Lasts.* (Chicago, IL: Northfield Publishing, 2015), 18.

2. JoAnn Grif Alspach, "Loneliness and Social Isolation: Risk Factors Long Overdue for Surveillance." *Critical Care Nurse* 1 December 2013; 33 (6): 8–13. doi: https://doi.org/10.4037/ccn2013377

3. Jay E. Adams, *Proverbs*, The Christian Counselor's Commentary (Cordova, TN: Institute for Nouthetic Studies, 2020), 140.

Chapter 7—Transition to Ministry

1. Gary R. Collins, Ph.D., *Christian Counseling: A Comprehensive Guide.* (Nashville, TN: Thomas Nelson, 2007), 466.

Chapter 8—Trust the Transition Process

1. Gary Chapman, *The 5 Love Languages: The Secret to Love That Lasts.* (Chicago, IL: Northfield Publishing, 2015), 92.

2. James Strong, *New Strong's Exhaustive Concordance of the Bible.* (Nashville, TN: Thomas Nelson Publishers, 1980), H5526.

3. Derek Kidner, *Psalms 73–150: An Introduction and Commentary*, vol. 16, Tyndale Old Testament Commentaries (Downers Grove, IL: InterVarsity Press, 1975), 364.

Chapter 9—Overcome Fear

1. Cliff Kvidahl, "Timothy," ed. John D. Barry et al., *The Lexham Bible Dictionary* (Bellingham, WA: Lexham Press, 2016).

2. Max Anders, *Galatians-Colossians*, vol. 8, Holman New Testament Commentary (Nashville, TN: Broadman & Holman Publishers, 1999), 262.

3. John R. W. Stott, *The Letters of John: An Introduction and Commentary*, vol. 19, Tyndale New Testament Commentaries (Downers Grove, IL: InterVarsity Press, 1988), 169.

4. Jay E. Adams, *The Christian Counselor's New Testament and Proverbs*, ed. Donn R. Arms, Fourth Revised Edition. (Cordova, TN: Institute for Nouthetic Studies, 2019), 494.

Chapter 10—Find Freedom

1. Jill Savage, *Empty Nest, Full Life Discovering God's Best for Your Next*. (Chicago, IL: Moody Publishers, 2019), 79.

2. Smitha Bhandari. "Positive Thinking: What It Is and How to Do It." WebMD, January 16, 2018. https://www.webmd.com/mental-health/positive-thinking-overview#3.

3. Shahram Heshmat, Ph.D., "Basics of Identity," *Psychology Today*, December 08, 2014.

4. Sonja Haller. "Meet the 'lawnmower parent,' the new helicopter parents of 2018." *USA Today*, Sept. 20, 2018. https://www.usatoday.com/story/life/allthemoms/2018/09/19/meet-lawnmower-parent-new-helicopter-parents-types-parents-tiger-attachment/1347358002/

Chapter 11—Self-Care During Transition

1. Katie Thompson. "More Americans than Ever Are Caregivers for Ailing, Aging Loved Ones." WCVB, February 17, 2023. https://www.wcvb.com/article/more-americans-caregivers-ailing-aging-loved-ones/42954205.

Chapter 12—Accept A New Season

1. Marilyn Murray Willison. "Widow Facts, by Marilyn Murray Willison." | Creators Syndicate, August 18, 2017. https://www.creators.com/read/positive-aging/08/17/widow-facts.

2. Tony Evans. *The Tony Evans Bible Commentary*. 1st ed. (Nashville: Holman Bible Publisher, 2019), 1265.

3. Kathleen M. Rehl, Ph.D., CFP. *Moving Forward on Your Own: A Financial Guidebook for Widows*. (Land O Lakes, FL: Rehl Financial Advisors, 2015), 14.

Chapter 13—Clarity in Transition

1. Jay E. Adams, *Romans, Philippians, I Thessalonians, and II Thessalonians*, The Christian Counselor's Commentary (Cordova, TN: Institute for Nouthetic Studies, 2020), 71.

2. Max Anders, *Galatians-Colossians*, vol. 8, Holman New Testament Commentary (Nashville, TN: Broadman & Holman Publishers, 1999), 264.

3. Trevor Hudson. *The Serenity Prayer: A Simple Prayer to Enrich Your Life*. (Nashville, TN: The Upper Room Books, 2012), 16.

ABOUT THE AUTHOR

Dr. Evelyn Johnson-Taylor is an award-winning author, speaker, coach, mentor, ordained elder, and theology professor. Evelyn has been a women's ministry leader for more than thirty years. She served with her late husband as the founding pastors of three congregations. Evelyn also served as president of Women of Promise International Ministries Inc., a nonprofit offering hope and healing to women.

Evelyn holds an associate degree in nursing, a Bachelor of Arts in Women's Studies, and master's and PhD degrees in ministry.

Serving as an advisory board member for Senior Connection Center Inc., with a focus on caregiver needs, she passionately volunteers her time. Over a decade, she devoted herself to caring for her husband amid his illness. Evelyn's advocacy for self-care serves as a powerful reminder, inspiring caregivers and emphasizing the significance of recognizing their own value.

Her overarching goal is to motivate and empower women, providing them with the necessary resources and support for thriving.

Evelyn finds joy in exploring unfamiliar destinations and spending time with her loved ones. She aspires to be a beacon of guidance for those navigating challenges. Drawing upon her personal experiences, she aims to inspire others with a source of encouragement and resilience.

She is a member of the Advanced Writers and Speakers Association, Christian Women Speakers, and Word Weavers International.

Connect with Dr. Evelyn Johnson-Taylor:

At www.evelynjtaylor.org,

Facebook: https://www.facebook.com/drevelyn.taylor, https://www.facebook.com/drevelynjohnsontaylor,

https://www.facebook.com/groups/275799153135504

https://www.facebook.com/groups/673983923100170, https://www.facebook.com/groups/186909589172543

X: @evelynjtaylor

Instagram: evelynjtaylor

Tik ToK: @evelynjtaylor07

LinkedIn: https://www.linkedin.com/in/evelyn-johnson-taylor-ph-d-590b513/

YouTube Channel: https://bit.ly/4b3poO

www.ingramcontent.com/pod-product-compliance
Lightning Source LLC
Chambersburg PA
CBHW062219080426
42734CB00010B/1957